Samsung Galaxy S23 Ultra

Easy-to-Follow Manual with Useful
Samsung Galaxy S23 Ultra Hidden Features and Unlocking the Potential of
Your Device

Ernest
Woodruff

Table of Contents

INTRODUCTION

The new Galaxy S23 Ultra is not exactly revolutionary, which is no surprise given the introduction of the S22 Ultra. Instead, it seems virtually precisely the same as its predecessor, complete with the angular edges that have become its trademark. Moreover, you still have access to the reliable S Pen and the remarkable 10X optical zoom camera.

But, despite its similarities to its predecessor, the newly released S23 Ultra improves upon several core aspects essential to a fantastic flagship smartphone. The new 200-megapixel primary camera, which promises print-worthy quality in your images and much improved night shots, has had to be the most significant improvement this year.

Also, it represents a change in strategy for Samsung. The company used to equip overseas versions of this phone with its in-house Exynos chip, which was a practice that many people condemned because those chips were just not as good as the Snapdragon processors used in the U.S. models. However, beginning with the S23 Ultra, all versions of this phone, regardless of where they are sold, are equipped with the same powerful Snapdragon chip.

Galaxy S23 Ultra: Snapdragon versus Exynos

Samsung has made it easy to choose the Galaxy S23 model most suited to your needs. If you don't use an S Pen, the Galaxy S23 Plus model is much lighter-weight and less expensive than the Ultra variant. Nevertheless, the Ultra model is better if you use an S Pen. The S23 Plus does not come with a camera with an optical zoom of 10 times, but it does have a camera with three times. It also has the same CPU, charging rates, and a smaller battery than the S23.

The Galaxy S23 Ultra is the best option for those individuals who want a more compact smartphone.

The fact that the Snapdragon 8 Gen 2 CPU will be included in all Galaxy S23 Ultra variants, notwithstanding the market in which they are sold, is excellent news for customers, as we have previously noted. The previous model's Exynos processor did not have the same level of power efficiency as the new one, and it even affected the picture quality. This issue will no longer be a concern with the new model.

CHAPTER ONE

Features of the Galaxy S23 Ultra

The Samsung Galaxy S23 Ultra is the company's most recent and cutting-edge flagship phone, with several innovative new features. It seems that Samsung's strategy for the device is very straightforward: improve upon the S22 Ultra in all areas in which it excelled and highlight those areas in particular.

While the S23 Ultra does not seem to be much different from its predecessor's outside design, the device's internal components have been significantly improved. Here, we'll look at some of the most notable features of the S23 Ultra and determine whether or not it's worth it to make a move.

1. A New Main Camera With 200 Megapixels

The Galaxy S23 Ultra is the first flagship device from Samsung to include a camera with a resolution of 200 megapixels. In addition, Samsung claims its newly developed ISOCELL HP2 sensor would provide dramatically improved low-light performance, enhanced dynamic range, and increased clarity levels.

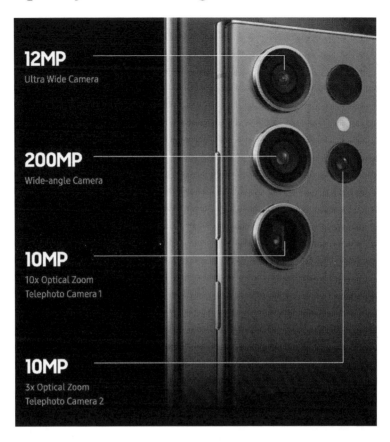

You can select a resolution between 12 megapixels, 50 megapixels, and 200 megapixels. One with a more excellent resolution is better suited for shooting during the day, while another with a lower resolution uses pixel-binning technology to capture images in low-light conditions. However, it is important to remember that switching to the 200MP mode will significantly increase the shutter latency, making it less suitable for recording fast-moving subjects.

Remember that the greatest resolution that a sensor can capture will only rise proportionally as the number of pixels increases. Therefore, even after increasing the magnification, the details in your photograph will remain intact; nevertheless, this does not guarantee an improvement in the quality of the picture as a whole.

Factors like color science, dynamic range, and shutter speed are determined by the algorithms used for picture processing, the chipset, and how well everything is tuned. Also, a higher-quality picture will need more space to save it.

2. Improved Videography

In addition to shooting better photographs, the device can now record films in both 4K portrait mode (also known as cinematic video) and uncropped 8K at 30 frames per second. In addition, the primary camera now incorporates Optical Image Stabilization with a corrective angle two times wider than before, which helps to decrease camera tremors.

Samsung's image-processing algorithms for low-light films have been fine-tuned to eliminate noise, overexposure, and excessive color saturation. These issues were among the most common criticisms against the S22 Ultra's low-light video capabilities. In addition, a brand-new mode called Astro Hyperlapse enables users to record time-lapse recordings of the night sky.

3. Custom-made chip based on the Snapdragon 8 Gen 2

The Galaxy S23 Ultra has the most recent Snapdragon 8 Gen 2 processor. As a result, it offers a performance increase of 34% for the central processing unit (CPU), 41% for the graphics processing unit (GPU), and 49% for the neural processing unit (NPU). Nevertheless, there is a catch.

The Snapdragon chip housed inside the S23 Ultra is unlike any other. In collaboration with Qualcomm, Samsung has developed an overclocked variant of the new chip exclusive to Galaxy devices called the **"Snapdragon 8 Gen 2 Mobile Platform for Galaxy."** This chip is only available in the S23 Ultra.

Even though it has such a terrible moniker, the S23 Ultra may have a slight advantage over other Android flagships now available on the market that contain the same processor, at least in terms of the scores it receives on benchmarks.

In addition, Samsung will discontinue production of its own Exynos CPUs and instead rely only on Qualcomm's Snapdragon processors for all S23 models sold around the globe. This is excellent news because Exynos processors are often known for having inferior performance than their Snapdragon competitors. So today, regardless of where you choose to make your purchase, every S23 device will provide the same level of performance.

4. Faster Storage and Memory

The Galaxy S23 series is now quicker and more responsive than ever, thanks to the most recent iteration of the UFS 4.0 storage standard and LPDDR5X RAM. This is a significant development since UFS 4.0 provides double the read and write speeds of its predecessor, UFS 3.1, and is 46% more efficient than its predecessor.

This implies that the S23 Ultra can access and save large files twice as quickly as the S22 Ultra while using significantly less battery life. At least, in principle, this is the case. However, for the age of 5G and upcoming VR technologies, UFS 4.0 will be an absolute need.

In addition, the highest speed that can be reached with LPDDR5X RAM is 8.5 Gbps, while its predecessor could only get 6.4 Gbps. Therefore, your phone's quality and clock speed matter a lot more than just having more RAM; this is one of the reasons why iPhones utilize less RAM than other smartphones while having more RAM available.

5. 256GB Basic Storage

The storage capacity of the Galaxy S23 Ultra begins at 256 gigabytes rather than the more typical 128 gigabytes. This will come in handy if you want to carry your phone about for an extended time, take many images, record films in 8K resolution, download movies and graphics-intensive games, and so on.

To clarify, 128 gigabytes of storage space is sufficient for most people; nevertheless, it is in no way sufficient for a phone intended for intensive usage and media consumption. As a result, it was a wise choice to make the storage capacity of the most basic model, 256 gigabytes, and the most advanced model, 1 terabyte.

6. Gorilla Glass Victus 2 Protection

Both the front and the rear of the Galaxy S23 Ultra have been outfitted with the most recent generation of Gorilla Glass, known as Victus 2. According to sources, the glass can survive fall of up to one meter on surfaces as tough as concrete and up to two meters on conditions that replicate asphalt's abrasiveness.

This means that even if you are one of the few individuals who do not use a case or screen protector on your smartphone, you can have peace of mind knowing that your device will be protected from damage caused by accidental drops.

7. Many More Minor Improvements

Also, several less significant enhancements ought to be brought to your attention. To begin, the quality of the loudspeakers has been substantially increased, and they now have a broader and clearer sound. In addition, the size of the vapor chamber has been expanded somewhat to improve the cooling capabilities when the user is gaming.

In addition, Samsung is collaborating with various app developers to improve the performance of popular social networking applications and games on Galaxy phones. As a result, you won't get the same generic experience you would get from using any other Android phone.

The more efficient processor should also result in a marginal improvement to the device's battery life. And as a last point, Samsung is boosting its usage of recycled materials to make parts of the components of Galaxy smartphones, including the front and back glass. This is done to reduce the company's impact on the environment.

Specifications

Model name: Samsung Galaxy S23 Ultra

Display type: Dynamic AMOLED 2X, 120Hz, HDR10+, 1200 nits (HBM), 1750 nits (peak)

Size: 6.8 inches

Protection: Corning Gorilla Glass Victus 2 Always-on display

OS: One UI 5.1, Android 13

Weight: 234g

Dimensions: 163.4 x 78.1 x 8.9mm

Chipset: Qualcomm SM8550-AC Snapdragon 8 Gen 2

Sensors: Accelerometer, proximity, gyro, Fingerprint (under the display, ultrasonic), compass, barometer

Battery: Li-Ion 5000 mAh non-removable

Charging: 45W wired, PD3.0, 65% in 30 mins

Colors: Green, Phantom black, green, graphite., sky blue. Lavender, red, lime.

USB: USB type 3.2, OTG

Main Camera: 200 MP, f/1.7, 24mm (wide), 10x optical zoom, 1/1.3", multi-directional PDAF, Laser AF, OIS 10 MP, f/4.9, 230mm (periscope telephoto), Dual Pixel PDAF, OIS

Selfie Camera: Dual pixel PDAF, 12 MP, f/2.2, 26mm (wide)

Samsung Galaxy S23 Ultra Description

Design, Colors, and the S Pen on the Galaxy S23 Ultra

The Galaxy S23 Ultra is similar to its predecessor in that it has angular edges, but it differs from the iPhone in that it has flatter sides. As a result, it's sort of like having the best of both worlds. It still has a slightly curved screen, but Samsung has made minor improvements, such as making the power and volume buttons slightly larger and moving them somewhat lower for easy access. Moreover, the cameras on the device's rear have been significantly upgraded.

It is still composed of glass and metal, but the back is made of Corning's new Gorilla Glass Victus 2, designed to be more resilient if the device is dropped. The middle frame is still made of aluminum. The IP68 classification for protection against water and dust has not been updated by Samsung, although it is already the highest possible grade.

In terms of the color options for the Galaxy S23 Ultra, the following is offered:

The four palette colors are Phantom Black, Cotton Flower, Mystic Lilac, and Botanic Green.

Also, Samsung's website has a selection of unique colors for specific products.

Last but most certainly not least, the S Pen is still included in the package for the S23 Ultra. It maintains the same appearance and feels as previously, and this front has no additional functionality.

Galaxy S23 Ultra Display

It should come as no surprise, given Samsung's position as the industry leader in display technology, that the screen on the S23 Ultra looks excellent; yet, the screen on the S22 Ultra also looked wonderful.

The fundamentals have remained the same from the previous year, including the max brightness of 1,750 nits, the same 1440p resolution, and the same LTPO technology enabling a variable refresh rate that ranges from 1Hz to 120Hz. The screen now has a new setting that allows for a significant reduction in brightness, making it ideal for usage in the evening.

For everything else, it has the same large 6.8-inch screen but with a wider aspect ratio than is typical.

Regarding its biometric capabilities, the S23 Ultra retains the tried-and-true ultrasonic fingerprint scanner that Qualcomm manufactured. This scanner is renowned for its lightning-fast processing times and high dependability. Moreover, the front-facing camera of the device can do image-based facial recognition. Nevertheless, picture recognition is a tremendous pain when it's nighttime. Since the phone automatically adjusts the brightness to a very high level to detect your face, which may be uncomfortable at night, we were compelled to disable that option.

Galaxy S23 Ultra Camera

The S23 Ultra quad camera has one significant enhancement over its predecessor as well as a few others of a less substantial kind. Still, on the whole, it is not a significantly different camera system.

After employing a sensor with 108 megapixels as the primary camera for the last three years, Samsung has decided to upgrade to an astounding new sensor with 200 megapixels. 200 megapixels seems ridiculous. Even while this is the case, the reason you should be amazed is not just due to the attention to detail. Most users may never really utilize the entire resolution. By default, Samsung uses pixel binning, which combines 16 pixels into one super-pixel so that you still get 12MP photographs even when you don't use the full resolution. But, since Samsung uses a technique known as pixel binning, the company can eliminate noise and produce remarkable nighttime photographs.

In addition, the ExpertRAW mode is now fully built directly into the camera app for enthusiasts. ExpertRAW on the S23 Ultra is more powerful than the ordinary **"Pro" mode** since it provides you with manual camera settings and allows you to shoot RAW files with multi-frame exposures. In other words,

ExpertRAW gives you more creative control over your photos. A 50-megapixel RAW file option is all new for this year, and although it won't use as much storage as a 200-megapixel file would, it still delivers a great deal more information than the standard 12-megapixel photo would.

The following is a brief rundown of the S23 Ultra camera's many features:

- 200MP main camera with a 23mm f/1.7 lens and enhanced optical image stabilization
- 12 megapixels ultra-wide, 13 mm, f/2.2
- 10 megapixels three times the zoom, f/2.4
- 10 megapixels, ten times the zoom, f/4.9
- 12 megapixels front camera

Samsung Galaxy S23 Ultra Performance

As indicated before, all the S23 versions are equipped with the Snapdragon 8 Gen 2 processor. To be more specific, it is a slightly modified version of the Snapdragon 8 Gen 2 processor that has been set to a higher clock speed to accommodate Samsung. This chip, on the other hand, is an absolute monster.

Performance Standards and Measures

Even while the processor is capable of supporting fancy new technologies like Wi-Fi 7 and 4K120 video, not these features make it into the Galaxy, and these two do not. The S23 Ultra still only supports Wi-Fi 6E and can capture videos in 4K at 60 frames per second, so there's that.

What is particularly amazing about Samsung's S23 Ultra is the company's choice to increase the basic model's storage capacity by 100% while maintaining the same pricing (at least in the U.S.). These are the several models that may be purchased:

- 8GB RAM + 256GB storage
- 12GB RAM + 512GB storage

- 12 GB of RAM and one Terabyte of storage

It's terrific that there's an option for 1 terabyte of storage for advanced users. Still, the effect of offering 256 gigabytes as the standard model will be far bigger for the average user.

Before the launching of the S23 Ultra, there were rumors that it would include a satellite connection, exactly like the iPhone 14 series, but sadly, this is NOT the case.

Galaxy S23 Ultra Android version

On top of Android 13, the newest version of Samsung's One UI, version 5.1, is installed on the S23 Ultra. This interface is designed in the typical Samsung fashion and includes no significant new features.

One UI 5.1 has a more polished appearance than previous versions, and finally, a significant portion of the microjitter that was previously present has been eliminated. This is an excellent accomplishment for Samsung.

If you access the system settings, you can discover that it indicates the operating system uses up to 60 GB of space. This is something that you should be aware of. You should be aware that this is not the case, and that number is deceptive.

There is a "loss" of storage that cannot be avoided due to a mismatch in how computers calculate storage (1 GB of storage is somewhere about 1.073 GB in binary). For example, the storage type we refer to as 512 gigabytes only has around 494 gigabytes of available capacity. However, Samsung includes that disparity in the **"system"** size figure, which increases the system size number. Instead of factoring that discrepancy out, Samsung has it.

But Samsung's dedication to long-term support is the feature that stands out the most about the software for the S23 series. As a result, the S23 series will get four years' worth of major upgrades and five years' worth of security updates, which is more than even Google provides for its Pixel phones.

Galaxy S23 Ultra Battery

The battery life of the S23 Ultra has increased even though it has the same 5,000 mAh capacity as the battery included in last year's model.

Regarding audio playback time, Samsung estimates that the S23 Ultra will last 99 hours, 22% longer than the model from the previous year. According to the official numbers provided by Samsung, the new S23 Ultra can provide up to 27 hours of video playback, which is a 30% improvement over the S22 Ultra. Those upgrading from an older model with an Exynos processor will see an even more significant boost.

Samsung Galaxy S23 Ultra Charging

Speeds

The charging structure, on the other hand, has not been updated.

The S23 Ultra supports the same 45-watt charging with a cable as it was previously. Moreover, much as in prior years, the package only contains a wire, not a console charger. These speeds are adequate, but compared to those supported by other firms, which may be up to twice as fast, they are a bit of a letdown. Although the other competitors can now obtain a full charge in less than half an hour or even faster, the S23 Ultra will still need more than an hour.

Additionally, remember that to get those 45-watt rates, you will need to combine Samsung's 45W charger with a unique USB-C connection that provides 5A. (thicker than the average USB-C cable).

Moreover, the S23 Ultra can wirelessly charge at rates of up to 10W. When other devices are placed on its back, it can perform a process known as reverse wireless charging (you could top up wireless headphones, a smartphone, or another phone, for example). Intriguingly, Samsung decided to scale down the wireless charging rate since the last Samsung phones enabled quicker, 15W wireless charging rates.

Haptics and Ultra-High Audio Quality on the Galaxy S23 Ultra

Compared to the previous year's model, the loudspeaker quality found in the S23 Ultra represents a significant upgrade. The sound comes through with far more force than it did with the previous model, which did not reach nearly as loud. However, this is not simply a matter of volume; the sound produced by the S22 Ultra is not very clear, there is almost no depth to it, and the drums have a muffled quality. In contrast, the sound produced by the S23 Ultra is much cleaner; voices come through nice and clear with much less compression, and even when the volume is turned up to its maximum level, there is not much distortion. And maybe, most crucially, you can truly hear those lows, resulting in a far more robust sound profile.

The sound quality of the Galaxy S23 Ultra is somewhat superior to that of the Google Pixel 7 Pro, giving it the edge in this comparison. But, the Pixel is not quite as subpar as the S22 Ultra from the previous year, so the gap is not quite as large. In addition, the new S23 Ultra produces voices that are a little bit clearer than the Pixel, and it has a little more bass than the Pixel. But, again, the overall sound profile is much richer, which is immediately noticeable.

How to set up your Galaxy S23 Ultra

Congratulations on getting your new Samsung Galaxy S23 Ultra.

Here's a step-by-step guide on how to set up your device:

1. Turn on your Galaxy S23 Ultra by pressing and holding the power button on the phone's right side.

2. Follow the on-screen instructions to select your language, agree to the terms and conditions, and connect to Wi-Fi.

3. Sign in to your Google account or create a new one. This will allow you to access the Google Play Store, Gmail, and other Google services.

4. Next, set up biometric security options like facial recognition, fingerprint scanning, or a PIN.

5. Restore your apps and data from a previous device or backup by selecting **"Restore data"** during setup. Alternatively, you can set up your phone as a new device.

6. Customize your home screen by choosing your preferred wallpaper, widgets, and app icons. You can also rearrange the home screen by pressing and holding an app icon and moving it to a new location.

7. Download and install any additional apps from the Google Play Store.

8. Set up Samsung Pay if you plan to use it for mobile payments.

9. Set up Samsung DeX to connect your phone to a larger display.

10.   Finally, explore your new phone and get familiar with its features, such as the camera, Bixby voice assistant, and Samsung Health.

How to power on/off your device

To power on your Galaxy S23 Ultra:

1. Locate the power button on the right-hand side of your phone.

2. Press and hold the power button until the Samsung logo appears on the screen.

3. Once the logo appears, release the power button, and your phone will boot up.

To power off your Galaxy S23 Ultra:

1. Press and hold the power button until the power menu appears on the screen.

2. Tap **"Power off"** on the menu.

3. Tap **"Power off"** again on the confirmation prompt.

4. Wait for your phone to shut down completely.

Alternatively, you can use the Bixby voice assistant or the **"Device Care"** feature to power off your Galaxy S23 Ultra. To use Bixby, say, **"Hey Bixby, power off my phone" or "Hey Bixby, restart my phone" to** restart it. To use Device Care, go to **Settings > Device Care > and tap "Power off and restart."**

Transferring from an old device to a new device

Transferring data from an old device to a new one, like the Galaxy S23 Ultra, can be straightforward.

Here are the steps you can follow:

1. **Back up your old device:** The first step is to back up your old device. You can do this using Samsung Smart Switch, a built-in app that allows you to transfer data between Samsung devices. You can also use other backup methods, such as Google backup,

Samsung Cloud, or third-party backup software.

2. **Turn on your Galaxy S23 Ultra:** Turn on your new Galaxy S23 Ultra and follow the initial setup process. *(NB: Ensure you have a stable internet connection and your device is fully charged).*

3. **Connect your devices:** Once your new Galaxy S23 Ultra is set up, connect your old device using a USB cable and an adapter. You can also use Samsung Smart Switch wireless transfer option if your old device is compatible. Follow the prompts on your new device to connect to your old device.

4. **Select what to transfer:** On your new Galaxy S23 Ultra, you can select what you want to transfer. You can choose to transfer contacts, photos, messages, apps, and other data. Select the data you want to transfer and wait for the process to complete.

5. **Verify the transfer:** Once complete, verify that all your data has been transferred correctly. Check your contacts, photos, messages, and apps to ensure everything is working correctly.

Get started with Smart Switch

We use the Smart Switch app to copy your apps and data from your old device.

 By continuing, you agree to the **Terms and Conditions**.

Check our **Privacy Notice** to see how we manage your data, and allow the required **permissions**, including the permission below:

Device logs and usage data access
Used to optimise restored apps and to send log files to Samsung, including from third-party apps on your phone, to analyse issues when restoring apps

Deny

6. **Disconnect your devices:** Once you have verified the transfer, disconnect your devices by unplugging the USB cable.

By following these steps, you should be able to transfer all your data from your old device to your new Galaxy S23 Ultra with no issues.

CHAPTER TWO

How to insert SIM cards

To insert SIM cards into your Galaxy S23 Ultra, please follow these steps:

1. Locate the SIM tray on the top of your phone, near the edge.

2. Use the SIM ejection tool provided in the box or a paper clip to eject the SIM tray. Insert the tool into the small hole in the SIM tray.

3. Gently push the tool until the SIM tray pops out.

4. Remove the SIM tray from the phone.

5. If you have a dual-SIM version of the Galaxy S23 Ultra, you will see two slots on the tray labeled **"SIM 1" and "SIM 2."** If you have a single-SIM version, you will only see one slot.

6. Place the SIM card(s) in the slot(s), ensuring that the metal contacts are facing down and the notched corner is aligned with the notch on the tray.

7. Push the SIM tray back into the phone until it clicks into place.

8. Power on your phone and check if the SIM card(s) are detected.

Note: If you're having trouble ejecting the SIM tray, try pressing the tool harder or using a different tool. Don't use too much force, as this may damage your phone.

Making use of the Lift to Wake feature

The Lift to Wake feature on the Samsung Galaxy S23 Ultra is a convenient way to quickly access your phone's lock screen without having to press any buttons. To use this feature, follow these steps:

1. Go to your phone's settings menu.

2. Scroll down and select **"Advanced features."**

3. Tap on **"Motions and gestures."**

4. Toggle on **"Lift to wake."**

Once this feature is turned on, you can simply lift your phone to wake the screen and view your lock screen. This feature can save you time and effort when you need to quickly check your phone for notifications or the time.

It's important to note that the Lift to Wake feature may use more battery power, as it requires the phone to be constantly monitoring for motion. If you notice a significant decrease in battery life after enabling this feature, you may want to consider turning it off.

How to lock/unlock your device

To lock your Samsung Galaxy S23 Ultra, you can use one of the following methods:

Method 1: Press the power button on the side of the phone. *(NB: This will turn off the screen and lock the device).*

Method 2: Swipe down from the top of the screen to open the Quick Settings panel. Tap the lock icon to lock the device.

Method 3: Go to the **Settings app > Display > Lock screen**. Toggle on the **"Lock instantly with power key" option**. Now you can lock the device by pressing the power button.

To unlock your Samsung Galaxy S23 Ultra, you can use one of the following methods:

Method 1: Press the power button to turn on the screen. Then swipe up from the bottom of the screen to unlock the device.

Method 2: Use the fingerprint scanner or facial recognition to unlock the device. To set up these features, go to the **Settings app > Biometrics and security > Biometrics**.

Method 3: Enter your PIN, password, or pattern to unlock the device.

Auto restart your device

You can enable auto restart on your Samsung Galaxy S23 Ultra to help keep your device running smoothly. Auto restart will automatically restart your device once a week, which can help to clear out any temporary files or processes that may be causing issues.

To enable auto restart on your Samsung Galaxy S23 Ultra, follow these steps:

1. Open the **Settings app**.

2. Scroll   down   and   select   **"General management"**.

3. Tap **"Reset"**.

4. Select **"Auto restart"**.

5. Toggle the switch to **"On"**.

6. Choose the day and time you want your device to restart each week.

7. Tap **"Done"** to save your settings.

Once you've enabled auto restart, your device will automatically restart at the time you've chosen each week. This can help to keep your device running smoothly and prevent any potential issues from occurring.

CHAPTER THREE

Customize Home Screen and Lock

Screens

To customize your home screen and lock screen on your Samsung Galaxy S23 Ultra, follow these steps:

1. Long-press on an empty area of your home screen to bring up the customization options.

2. From here, you can customize your wallpaper by tapping on **"Wallpapers"**.

3. You can choose from preloaded wallpapers, or you can use your own photo by tapping on **"My photos"**.

4. You can also customize the layout of your home screen by selecting **"Home screen settings"**.

5. In this menu, you can choose the grid size, icon size, and other options to customize your home screen to your liking.

6. To customize your lock screen, go to **Settings > Lock screen**.

7. From here, you can change your lock screen wallpaper, add or remove widgets, and customize the clock style and other options.

8. You can also enable features like Always On Display to show information on your lock screen even when your phone is locked.

9. Once you've customized your home screen and lock screen, be sure to tap **"Apply" or "Save"** to save your changes.

With these customization options, you can make your Samsung Galaxy S23 Ultra truly your own and tailor it to your preferences.

How to add custom widgets to the Home Screen

To add custom widgets to the Home Screen of your Samsung Galaxy S23 Ultra, follow these steps:

1. Press and hold on any empty space on the Home Screen until the options menu appears.

2. Tap on **"Widgets"** from the menu.

3. Scroll through the list of available widgets until you find the one you want to add.

4. Press and hold on the widget you want to add, then drag it to the desired location on the Home Screen.

5. Release your finger to drop the widget in place.

If you can't find the widget you want to add, you may need to download it from the Google Play Store. Once you have downloaded and installed the widget, follow the steps above to add it to your Home Screen.

Customize notification features

To customize notification features on your Samsung Galaxy S23 Ultra, follow these steps:

1. Open the **"Settings" app** on your phone.

2. Scroll down and tap on **"Notifications."**

3. Here you will see a list of apps installed on your phone that have notification settings. Tap on the app you want to customize.

4. In the app's notification settings, you can choose whether to allow or block notifications from the app. You can also choose to show or

hide notifications on the lock screen or adjust the notification tone and vibration settings.

5. You can also tap on **"Advanced"** to see more options, including notification sound, vibration pattern, and notification style. You can even choose to show notifications as banners, pop-ups, or silently in the notification tray.

You can repeat these steps for each app you want to customize notification settings for. By customizing your notification settings, you can ensure that you only receive notifications that are important to you, and that they appear in a way that is convenient and useful.

Customize the edge screen display

You can choose to customize the edge screen display if you want. Here's how you can customize the edge screen display on your Samsung Galaxy S23 Ultra:

1. Open the Settings app on your phone.

2. Scroll down and tap on **Display**.

3. Tap on **Edge Screen**.

4. Here, you'll see several options to customize your edge screen display:

- **Edge panels:** This option allows you to choose which edge panels you want to appear when you swipe in from the edge of the screen. You can select from a variety of panels, including App Pair, People Edge, Smart Select, and more.

- **Edge lighting:** This option allows you to customize the lighting that appears around the edges of your phone when you receive notifications. You can choose the color, style, and duration of the lighting.

- **Edge touch:** This option allows you to choose what happens when you touch the edge of the screen. You can set it to launch an app, open a shortcut, or do nothing.

- **Edge panels handle:** This option allows you to adjust the size and position of the handle that appears on the edge of the screen when you swipe in.

5. Once you've made your desired changes, simply exit the settings app and your edge screen display will be customized according to your preferences.

Note: The edge screen display options may vary depending on your phone's software version and country of origin.

CHAPTER FOUR

The Samsung Galaxy Store

The Samsung Galaxy Store is a digital app store that comes pre-installed on Samsung devices, including the Galaxy S23 Ultra. It offers a wide range of apps, games, and other digital content for Samsung users to download and enjoy on their devices.

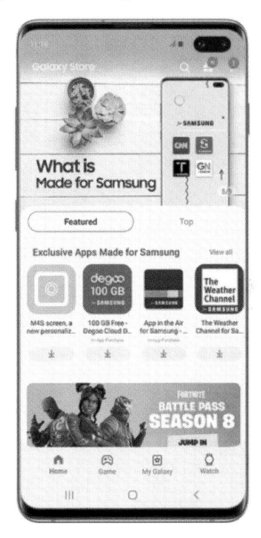

Here's some information on the Samsung Galaxy Store and how to use it on your Galaxy S23 Ultra:

1. **Finding and downloading apps:** You can access the Samsung Galaxy Store by tapping on its icon in your app drawer or by swiping up

from the bottom of the screen and tapping on the Galaxy Store icon. Once you're in the store, you can browse through the various categories of apps, games, and other digital content. You can also search for specific apps by typing in their names in the search bar at the top of the screen. To download an app, simply tap on its icon and then tap on the Install button.

2. **Managing your apps:** You can manage your installed apps by tapping on the three horizontal lines in the top left corner of the Galaxy Store screen and selecting My apps from the drop-down menu. Here, you can see a list of all the apps you've downloaded from the store, and you can update or uninstall them as needed.

3. **Samsung-exclusive apps:** The Samsung Galaxy Store also features a number of exclusive apps that are only available to Samsung users. These apps include Samsung

Health, Samsung Pay, and Samsung Members, among others.

4. **Deals and promotions:** The Samsung Galaxy Store often offers deals and promotions on apps, games, and other digital content. To see what deals are currently available, tap on the three horizontal lines in the top left corner of the Galaxy Store screen and select Deals from the drop-down menu.

Overall, the Samsung Galaxy Store is a convenient and easy-to-use app store that offers a wide range of digital content for Samsung users to enjoy on their Galaxy S23 Ultra devices.

Downloading and installing applications

The steps:

1. Open the **Play Store app** on your phone.

2. Look for the app you want to download using the search bar at the top of the screen.

Alternatively, you can browse through the different categories to find the app you want.

3. Once you have found the app you want to download, click on it to open its page.

4. Click the **"Install" button** to begin downloading and installing the app.

5. The app will be downloaded and installed on your Galaxy S23 Ultra automatically. *(NB: You can view the progress of the download in the notifications bar at the top of the screen).*

6. Once the download and installation are complete, you can find the app on your phone's home screen or in the app drawer.

If you have trouble downloading or installing an app, you can try the following troubleshooting steps:

1. **Check your internet connection:** Make sure your phone is connected to a stable internet

connection, either through Wi-Fi or mobile data.

2. **Clear the Google Play Store cache:** Go to **"Settings" > "Apps" > "Google Play Store" > "Storage" > "Clear Cache".**

3. **Restart your phone:** Sometimes restarting your phone can help fix issues with downloading or installing apps.

4. **Check for software updates:** Make sure your Galaxy S23 Ultra is up to date with the latest software updates. Go to **"Settings" > "Software update" > "Download and install".**

If none of these steps work, you can try contacting the app developer or Samsung support for further assistance.

Import and Export PDFs

You can now import PDF documents into the Samsung Notes app on your Galaxy S23 Ultra. You can annotate, write on, and draw on your PDFs directly in the app, then store them for later use. If you need to add the information to another document, there are other choices for exporting PDFs and notes, such as PowerPoint presentations or Microsoft Word documents.

It's worth noting that PDF files imported or exported from Samsung Notes can't be altered. The PDF may only include text and graphics. If you don't have the most current version of Samsung Notes, some of these capabilities may be grayed out or inaccessible.

Import a PDF document

You can import PDFs into Samsung Notes if you have them stored on your phone. Users can save the PDF for later or use your S Pen to add notes on it.

Note: When you import a PDF into Samsung Notes, it creates a duplicate of the original file. You may remove the original PDF file from My Files if you no longer need it.

- Open the Samsung Notes app and hit the **PDF icon** to begin importing a PDF file.
- After that, choose a folder and then your preferred PDF file. Don't forget to tap Done.
- You can now edit the file by adding text or graphics. You can rapidly convert your writing to text or straighten it if you're using the S Pen.
- Select the **Convert to text icon** to convert the writing to text. To convert everything to text, check the text preview and then hit **Convert**.

- Select the **Straighten icon** to straighten unconverted handwriting.
- When you're done, use the Back arrow to save the file.

Create a PDF document

Any note you write or change in Samsung notes may be exported as a PDF file, even one to which you've added notes.

- To export a note, launch the Samsung Notes app and choose the note you want to export.
- Then tap **Save as a file** from the **More options** (three vertical dots) menu.
- Select **PDF file**, then go to the location where you want to save the file. If you need to create a new folder, tap the + symbol. Tap Store after you've determined where you want to save the file

- The file will be stored in the format you specified to your device.
- Simply hit **More choices** (the three vertical dots) and then **Delete** if you no longer need the copy in Samsung Notes. After that, choose to **Move to Trash**.

How to use the contacts app

These are the actions that need to be taken in order to utilize the Contacts app on the Samsung Galaxy S23 Ultra:

1. Launch the Contacts application on your device. You may do this task by going to your home screen, pressing on the **"Phone" app**, and then choosing the **"Contacts" option** that is located at the bottom of the screen.

2. Tap the **"+" symbol** at the bottom of the screen to add a new contact to your address book. This will open a new contact screen for

you, where you may input the person's name, phone number, email address, and any other information that may be pertinent.

3. To make changes to an existing contact, choose the contact from the list by tapping on his or her name, and then select the pencil icon located in the top right corner of the screen. You can alter any of the contact's information as a result of doing this.

4. Tap the magnifying glass icon at the top of the screen to begin searching for a contact. After you have done so, you will be prompted to input either the name or the phone number of the person you are trying to find.

5. Just press and hold on the contact's name in the list, and when the menu that displays, pick **"Delete"** from the list. This will remove the contact.

6. You may also create a contact group in order to gather your contacts together. To do this, press the three dots that are located in the top right-hand corner of the screen, and from the menu that appears, pick **"Manage contacts."** You will then be able to add contacts to an existing group, create new groups, and manage your current contact groups from that location.

7. You can sync your contacts with your Google account or with other accounts, such as Microsoft Exchange or iCloud, using the Contacts app. This feature is also available to you. To do this, press the three dots located in the top right-hand corner of the screen, pick **"Settings,"** and then select **"Accounts and backup"** from the list of options that appears. You'll then be able to pick the account that you want to sync with and set the contact syncing options that you wish to use.

That was a quick rundown of the fundamentals involved in making use of the Contacts app on the Samsung Galaxy S23 Ultra. You won't ever have to worry about losing touch with the people who are most important to you thanks to this app's simple but effective contact management and organization features.

How to use the Notes app

You can write, edit, and arrange your notes on your Galaxy S23 Ultra with the help of the Samsung Notes app.

How to use the app is as follows:

1. Launch the **Samsung Notes application** on your device. You can do this by pressing on the app icon that is located on your home screen, or you can locate **"Samsung Notes"** in the app drawer by searching for it.

2. Tap the plus sign ('+') symbol located at the bottom of the screen to start a new note. *(NB: This will bring up a new note screen in which you may type in your notes, draw on them, add photos or music, etc).*

3. You can style your text by using the tools for formatting that are located at the top of the screen. These tools offer choices for bold, italic, underline, and bullet points, among other alternatives.

4. You also have the option to include videos, audio notes, and photographs inside your remark. To do this, first locate the **"Insert" symbol** in the formatting bar (it resembles a plus sign enclosed inside a circle), and then choose the kind of media that you want to include in the document.

5. Tap the symbol that looks like a pen in the toolbar above the note field if you wish to

write it by hand. This will bring up a set of tools for drawing, including an eraser, a color picker, and a slider for adjusting the size of the brush. You also have the option of converting your handwritten notes into typed text by using the handwriting recognition technology.

6. Tap the arrow to the back that is located in the upper left corner of the screen to save your message. Your message will be stored in its entirety automatically.

7. If you want to keep your notes organized, you may put them in folders that you create for that purpose. To do this, touch the symbol that looks like three horizontal lines in the top left-hand corner of the screen, and then pick the **"Folders" option** from the menu that appears. You have the ability to create a new folder, transfer notes to other folders, or remove folders from that location.

8. If you want to hunt for a particular note, you may do so by tapping on the magnifying glass icon that is located at the top of the screen, and then entering the terms that are relevant to your search.

9. The Samsung Notes app also has a sync option that enables you to access your notes from other devices. This feature is available for free. In order to make advantage of this function, you will first need to log in to your Samsung account and then activate the sync setting inside the app's configuration options.

Whether you're taking notes for work, school, or personal use, this software makes it simple to write, modify, and organize them all in a centralized location. You can use it for any purpose you need to take notes.

How to use the Calculator App

Follow these instructions on how to use the calculator application on your Galaxy S23 Ultra:

1. Swiping your finger upward from the bottom of the home screen will open the app drawer.

2. Locate the icon for the Calculator app and then touch on it.

3. The calculator app will launch, presenting the fundamental calculator with the addition, subtraction, multiplication, and division capabilities.

4. Tap the numbers and functions that are shown on the screen in order to make a computation.

5. Use the "C" button on your keyboard to clear the display.

6. Swipe from right to left on the screen to enter the scientific calculator, and then swipe again to reach the programmer mode. Using the advanced functions requires that you do this.

7. Swipe from left to right on the screen to return to the calculator's standard mode.

8. To make use of the memory feature, first press the "M" button to save the currently displayed value, and then press the "MR" button to retrieve the value that was previously saved.

Note: You can now execute a wide variety of computations on your Galaxy S23 Ultra by using the calculator application.

How to use the Map App

The Map app on the Samsung Galaxy S23 Ultra is a navigation program that delivers real-time traffic updates, turn-by-turn instructions, and other location-based services. The app is called **"Map."**

Follow these instructions in order to utilize the Map application on your Galaxy S23 Ultra:

1. Tap on the app's icon, either on the home screen or in the app drawer, to launch the **Map application**.

2. If asked, provide the app the permission to access your location.

3. You can enter your destination by pressing on the search box at the top of the page and entering in the address, name of the site, or even simply a category such as "coffee shops" or "gas stations." This will bring up a list of businesses that fit that category.

4. To reach your destination, choose the search result that best fits it.

5. When the route has been determined, the Map app will provide a map at the bottom of the screen that includes turn-by-turn instructions.

6. If you want to get at your location successfully, the app will give you with instructions.

7. By pressing your fingers together or spreading them out on the screen, you may zoom in or out of the map.

8. You can also change the perspective of the map by tapping on the three horizontal lines that are located in the upper left corner of the screen and choosing the view that you want.

9. To exit the navigation, you can do so by tapping the **"X" button** that is located in the upper-right hand corner of the screen.

The Map application that comes preinstalled on the Galaxy S23 Ultra has a number of new capabilities, including the capability to store and share locations, real-time traffic updates, and alternate routes.

How to use Samsung's built-in music app

The Samsung Music app is the built-in music player on the Samsung Galaxy S23 Ultra, and it allows you stream music from a variety of online sources in addition to playing music files that are saved locally on the device. The Samsung Music app may be used in the following ways:

1. Launch the **Samsung Music application** by touching its icon located either on the home screen or in the app drawer.

2. You will find a number of tabs on the main page, some of which are labeled **"My Files," "Playlists," "Albums," "Artists," "Folders," and**

"Tracks." Your music collection may be browsed and played in a variety of ways, all of which are accessible via these tabs.

3. To hear a song, you need just touch its name in the music list. The music will begin to play, and the playback controls can be found at the bottom of the screen. You may use these controls to regulate the playback.

4. Tap the **"Playlists" tab,** and then press the **"+"** **button** that is located in the top-right corner of the screen. This will allow you to create a new playlist. After that, you will be able to choose the songs that you wish to add to the playlist.

5. Tap the search symbol at the top of the screen and enter your search query to look for a certain song, artist, or album. You can find this button at the top of the screen.

6. Tap the menu button with three dots that is located in the upper-right corner of the screen, and then pick **"Settings"** from the drop-down menu that appears. You may make changes to settings like as the equalization, the sound effects, and the app notifications from this screen.

7. Also, a variety of online music streaming services, such as Spotify and YouTube Music, are supported through the Samsung Music app. To make use of any of these services, first click the **"Explore" option**, then touch on the one that most interests you.

Note: You can play and arrange your music collection on your Galaxy S23 Ultra using the Samsung Music app by following these simple instructions. Moreover, you can use the app to stream music from your preferred online music services.

Galaxy Wearable app

To use the Galaxy Wearable app on your Galaxy S23 Ultra, you can follow these instructions:

1. Launch the Google Play Store on your phone and seek the **"Galaxy Wearable"** app. Alternatively, you may obtain it directly from the Samsung Galaxy Store.

2. Download and install the app on your device.

3. Start the **Galaxy Wearable app** on your phone.

4. Ensure that your Galaxy S23 Ultra is linked to your Galaxy wearable device through Bluetooth or Wi-Fi.

5. Comply with the on-screen instructions to configure your device and personalize settings, such as notifications, apps, and watch faces.

6. After completing the setup, you may manage your wearable device using the Galaxy

Wearable app. This includes installing and updating applications, monitoring fitness and health statistics, and adjusting settings.

Note: The functionality available may vary depending on the wearable device you are using.

How to create and log into your Samsung account

To create and log into your Samsung account on Galaxy S23 Ultra, you can follow these steps:

Creating a Samsung Account:

1. Open the **"Settings" app** on your Galaxy S23 Ultra.

2. Scroll down and select **"Accounts and backup."**

3. Tap **"Accounts."**

4. Select **"Add Account."**

5. Choose **"Samsung account" and tap "Create Account."**

6. Enter your details and follow the on-screen instructions to create your Samsung account.

Logging into your Samsung Account:

1. Open the **"Settings" app** on your Galaxy S23 Ultra.

2. Scroll down and select **"Accounts and backup."**

3. Tap **"Accounts."**

4. Select **"Add Account."**

5. Choose **"Samsung account"** and enter your login credentials (email/phone number and password).

6. Tap **"Sign in"** to log into your Samsung account.

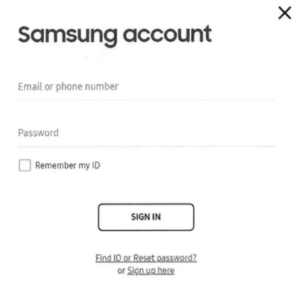

Once you have logged in, you can access and manage your Samsung account and its associated services and features from your Galaxy S23 Ultra.

Making use of Samsung Pay

To make use of Samsung Pay on your Galaxy S23 Ultra, you can follow these steps:

1. Ensure your device is connected to a mobile network or Wi-Fi.

2. Launch the Samsung Pay app. If it is not pre-installed on your device, you can download it from the Galaxy Store or Google Play Store.

3. Tap **"Add"** to add your payment card(s) to Samsung Pay. You can choose to add a credit or debit card, or a gift card.

4. Follow the on-screen instructions to verify your card. You may need to provide additional information such as your card details and billing address.

5. Once your card is verified, you can use Samsung Pay to make payments at supported merchants. To do this, swipe up from the bottom of the screen to access Samsung Pay, select the card you want to use, and place your phone near the payment terminal.

6. Follow the prompts on the payment terminal to complete your transaction.

Samsung Pay also offers additional features such as rewards programs, discounts, and coupons. You can access these by tapping the "Home" tab in the Samsung Pay app and exploring the available offers.

Note that Samsung Pay is not supported by all merchants, and some may require additional setup or verification steps. It is also important to keep your device and payment information secure by setting up a secure lock screen and using Samsung Pay only at trusted merchants.

What can you use the Samsung Pay to do?

Samsung Pay is a mobile payment service that allows users to make payments using their Samsung devices. On the Galaxy S23 Ultra, you can use Samsung Pay to:

1. **Make payments at physical stores:** You can use Samsung Pay to make payments at

physical stores by simply holding your Galaxy S23 Ultra near a compatible card reader.

2. **Make online payments:** Samsung Pay can also be used to make online payments by selecting Samsung Pay at checkout on participating websites.

3. **Pay with rewards points:** If you have accumulated rewards points on your Samsung account, you can use Samsung Pay to redeem them for purchases.

4. **Pay transit fares**: In some cities, you can use Samsung Pay to pay for transit fares by tapping your device on the transit card reader.

5. **Store loyalty and membership cards:** Samsung Pay also allows you to store and use your loyalty and membership cards, so you don't need to carry them around physically.

Note that the availability of Samsung Pay features may vary by region and device, so be sure to check if the service is available in your area and if your device is compatible.

What to do if Samsung Pay does not work

If Samsung Pay is not working on your Galaxy S23 Ultra, there are several things you can try:

1. **Check if Samsung Pay is compatible with your device:** Make sure your Galaxy S23 Ultra is compatible with Samsung Pay. Check if Samsung Pay is available in your region and if your device is supported.

2. **Check if your device is up to date:** Ensure that your Galaxy S23 Ultra is running the latest software update. To check for updates, go to **Settings > Software update > Download and install.**

3. **Check your internet connection:** Samsung Pay requires an internet connection to work.

Check if your Wi-Fi or mobile data is turned on and has a stable connection.

4. **Check if your payment card is supported:** Make sure the payment card you are trying to use is supported by Samsung Pay. Some banks and card issuers may not be supported.

5. **Check if you have set up Samsung Pay correctly:** Verify that you have set up Samsung Pay correctly. Open the Samsung Pay app and follow the on-screen instructions to add your payment card.

6. **Restart your device:** Try restarting your Galaxy S23 Ultra and see if Samsung Pay works afterward.

7. **Contact Samsung Support:** If the above steps do not work, contact Samsung Support for further assistance.

CHAPTER FIVE

Setting up Internet on your device

To set up internet on your Galaxy S23 Ultra, follow these steps:

1. Swipe down from the top of the screen to open the notification panel and then tap the gear icon to access the Settings menu.

2. Scroll down and tap **"Connections"** and then tap **"Mobile networks"**.

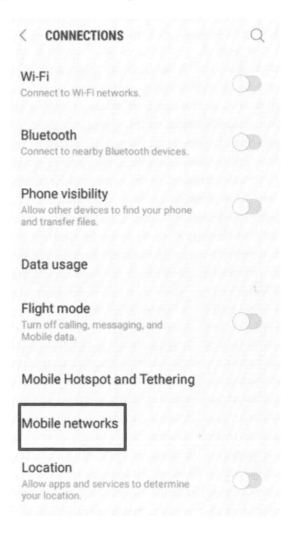

3. Tap **"Access Point Names" (APN)** and then tap the plus (+) sign to add a new APN.

4. Fill in the required information for your carrier's APN settings, which you can find on their website or by contacting their customer

support. The most important fields to fill in are the name, APN, username, and password.

5. Once you've entered all the required information, tap the three-dot icon in the top right corner and select **"Save"**.

6. Now, tap the newly created APN to make it the default, and your internet should now be set up on your Galaxy S23 Ultra.

If you're having trouble setting up your internet, you may need to restart your phone or contact your carrier for assistance.

How to connect to a Wi-Fi network

To connect to a Wi-Fi network on your Galaxy S23 Ultra, follow these steps:

1. Swipe down from the top of the screen to open the notification panel and then tap the Wi-Fi icon to turn on Wi-Fi.

2. Your phone will automatically search for available Wi-Fi networks. Tap on the Wi-Fi network you want to connect to.

3. If the Wi-Fi network is secured, you will need to enter the password to connect. Enter the password and then tap **"Connect"**.

4. Once your phone has successfully connected to the Wi-Fi network, the Wi-Fi icon in the notification panel will turn blue, and you should see the Wi-Fi network name at the top of your screen.

You can also add Wi-Fi networks manually by going to **"Settings" > "Connections" > "Wi-Fi" > "Add network"** and then entering the Wi-Fi network name and password.

If you're having trouble connecting to a Wi-Fi network, make sure your Wi-Fi is turned on, and you're within range of the network. You may also need to restart your phone or reset your Wi-Fi network settings.

How to use Bluetooth and other

connections

To use Bluetooth and other connections on your Galaxy S23 Ultra, follow these steps:

1. **Bluetooth:** To turn on Bluetooth, swipe down from the top of the screen to open the notification panel and then tap the Bluetooth icon. You can also turn on Bluetooth by going to **"Settings" > "Connections" > "Bluetooth"** and then toggling on the switch. Once Bluetooth is turned on, your phone will search for nearby devices. Tap on the device you want to pair with and follow the on-screen instructions to complete the pairing process.

2. **Wi-Fi Direct:** Wi-Fi Direct allows you to connect your phone directly to another device, such as a TV or computer, without a Wi-Fi network. To use Wi-Fi Direct, swipe down from the top

of the screen to open the notification panel and then tap the **"Quick settings" icon**. Tap **"Wi-Fi Direct"** and then select the device you want to connect to.

3. **NFC:** NFC (Near Field Communication) allows you to share content, such as photos or videos, with other NFC-enabled devices by simply tapping your phone against theirs. To use NFC, make sure NFC is turned on by going to **"Settings"** > **"Connections"** > **"NFC and payment"**. Then, hold the back of your phone against the back of the other NFC-enabled device to establish a connection.

4. **USB:** You can connect your phone to a computer or other device using a USB cable. Make sure USB Debugging is turned on by going **to "Settings"** > **"Developer options"** > **"USB Debugging"**. Then, connect your phone to the device using a USB cable.

5. **Smart View:** Smart View allows you to mirror your phone's screen on a compatible TV or other device. To use Smart View, swipe down from the top of the screen to open the notification panel and then tap the **"Smart View" icon**. Select the device you want to connect to and follow the on-screen instructions.

Note that the exact steps for using these connections may vary depending on your specific phone model and software version.

Connect to a nearby device scanning

How to scan for nearby devices using a Samsung Galaxy S23 Ultra:

1. Make sure that your device's Bluetooth is turned on. You can do this by swiping down from the top of the screen to access the Quick

Settings panel and tapping on the Bluetooth icon.

2. Open the Settings app on your Galaxy S23 Ultra.

3. Scroll down and tap on **"Connections."**

4. Tap on **"Bluetooth."**

5. Your device will automatically start scanning for nearby Bluetooth devices. The nearby devices will appear in a list under the **"Available devices" section**.

6. Tap on the name of the device you want to connect to.

7. Follow the on-screen instructions to complete the pairing process.

Note that the specific steps may vary depending on your device's software version and settings.

Connect with Mobile Hotspot

Here's how you can connect to a mobile hotspot on your Samsung Galaxy S23 Ultra:

1. Turn on the mobile hotspot on the device that you want to connect to. You can usually do this by going to the Settings app on that device, then finding and tapping on the **"Mobile hotspot" option**.

2. On your Galaxy S23 Ultra, swipe down from the top of the screen to access the Quick Settings panel.

3. Look for the **"Mobile hotspot" icon** and tap on it. If you don't see it, you can swipe left or right to find it.

4. Your Galaxy S23 Ultra will start scanning for available mobile hotspots. Once it finds the one you want to connect to, tap on it to connect.

5. If the mobile hotspot is password-protected, you'll need to enter the password to connect. You can usually find the password on the device that's broadcasting the mobile hotspot.

6. Once you've entered the password, tap **"Connect"** to connect to the mobile hotspot.

After you've connected, your Galaxy S23 Ultra will be able to access the internet through the mobile hotspot. Keep in mind that using a mobile hotspot can consume a lot of data, so be sure to keep track of your usage to avoid exceeding your data limit.

How to add Virtual Private Networks

Adding a Virtual Private Network (VPN) on your Samsung Galaxy S23 Ultra is a straightforward process.

Here's how you can do it:

1. Open the Settings app on your Galaxy S23 Ultra.

2. Scroll down and tap on **"Connections."**

3. Tap on **"More connection settings."**

4. Tap on **"VPN."**

5. Tap on the plus (+) icon in the top right corner to add a new VPN profile.

6. Enter the VPN's connection details, such as the VPN name, server address, and other settings provided by your VPN provider. You may also need to select the type of VPN you're using, such as PPTP or L2TP.

7. Once you've entered all the required details, tap **"Save"** to save the VPN profile.

8. Your newly created VPN profile will now be listed on the VPN screen. To connect to the VPN, simply tap on the profile.

9. You may be prompted to enter your VPN login credentials, such as your username and password.

10. After you've entered your login credentials, tap **"Connect"** to establish a VPN connection.

Once you've successfully connected to the VPN, a VPN icon will appear in the status bar at the top of your screen. This indicates that you're connected to the VPN and your internet traffic is encrypted and protected. To disconnect from the VPN, simply go back to the VPN screen and tap on the VPN profile, then tap **"Disconnect."**

CHAPTER SIX

Using S Pen

The S Pen is a stylus designed for use with Samsung Galaxy devices, including the Galaxy S23 Ultra. Here are some steps to help you get started using the S Pen with your Galaxy S23 Ultra:

1. **Ensure your device is compatible:** The S Pen is compatible with the Galaxy S23 Ultra, so make sure you have this device.

2. **Insert the S Pen:** The S Pen can be inserted into the designated slot on the bottom of your Galaxy S23 Ultra. Push the S Pen gently into the slot until it clicks into place.

3. **Use the S Pen:** Once the S Pen is inserted, you can use it to perform a variety of functions, including:

- **Writing and drawing:** Use the S Pen to write notes or draw on the screen of your Galaxy S23 Ultra.

- **Navigate:** You can use the S Pen to navigate the user interface of your device. Hover the S Pen over an item to see a preview, and click the button on the S Pen to select·it.

- **Take screenshots:** Press and hold the button on the S Pen while hovering over the screen to take a screenshot.

- **Air Actions:** With Air Actions enabled, you can use hand gestures to control your device. For example, you can flick your wrist to switch between front and back cameras or move your hand up and down to adjust the volume.

4. **Remove the S Pen:** To remove the S Pen, simply press on the end of the S Pen to release it from the slot.

Note: Be sure to store the S Pen in its designated slot when you're not using it. This will help prevent damage to the S Pen and your device.

How to configure the S Pen

You can configure your S Pen on your Galaxy S23 Ultra to customize its functions and settings.

Here are some steps to help you configure your S Pen:

1. **Open Settings:** Open the Settings app on your Galaxy S23 Ultra.

2. **Select Advanced Features:** Scroll down and select **"Advanced Features."**

3. **Select S Pen:** Under Advanced Features, select **"S Pen."**

4. **Customize S Pen functions:** In the S Pen settings menu, you can customize various S Pen functions, such as Air Actions, S Pen

Shortcuts, and S Pen Settings. Here are some options you can explore:

- **Air Actions:** This feature lets you perform actions by waving your S Pen in certain directions. You can customize the actions that correspond to each gesture, such as taking a screenshot or playing music.

- **S Pen Shortcuts:** You can set up shortcuts for various S Pen functions, such as creating a note or taking a screenshot. You can also add new shortcuts or remove existing ones.

- **S Pen Settings:** You can adjust various S Pen settings, such as the S Pen sensitivity and sound effects.

5. **Customize App Actions:** You can also customize what the S Pen does when using certain apps. For example, you can set up the

S Pen to launch specific apps or perform certain actions within an app.

6. **Save changes:** Once you have configured the S Pen settings to your liking, be sure to save your changes.

By following these steps, you can configure your S Pen on your Galaxy S23 Ultra to suit your preferences and make the most of its features.

How to charge the S Pen

The S Pen for the Galaxy S23 Ultra has a built-in battery that needs to be charged from time to time.

Here are some steps to help you charge the S Pen:

1. **Insert the S Pen:** Insert the S Pen into its designated slot on the bottom of your Galaxy S23 Ultra. *(NB: The S Pen should click into place).*

2. **Check the battery level:** You can check the battery level of your S Pen by going to the S Pen settings in your device's Settings app. If the battery level is low, you will need to charge the S Pen.

3. **Begin charging:** To begin charging the S Pen, leave it inserted into the device's slot. The S Pen will start charging automatically.

4. **Check the charging status**: You can check the charging status of the S Pen by going to the S Pen settings in your device's Settings app. The battery level will increase as the S Pen charges.

5. **Remove the S Pen:** Once the S Pen is fully charged, you can remove it from the device's slot. To remove the S Pen, press on the end of the S Pen to release it from the slot.

Note: The S Pen can also be charged wirelessly when it is placed on the back of the Galaxy S23 Ultra. To charge the S Pen wirelessly, make sure the device is connected to a wireless charger and place the S Pen on the back of the device.

By following these steps, you can charge the S Pen for your Galaxy S23 Ultra and keep it ready for use whenever you need it.

Taking photos with the S Pen

Yes, it is possible to take photos with the S Pen on the Galaxy S23 Ultra. The S Pen is a stylus that comes with some Samsung devices, including the Galaxy S23 Ultra. It can be used for various functions, including taking photos.

To take a photo with the S Pen on the Galaxy S23 Ultra, follow these steps:

1. Open the Camera app on your Galaxy S23 Ultra.

2. Hold the S Pen close to the phone's screen until the Air Command menu appears.

3. Select the **"Camera" option** from the Air Command menu.

4. Use the S Pen button to zoom in or out.

5. Press the S Pen button once to take a photo.

6. You can use the S Pen to edit the photo by selecting the **"Edit" option** from the Air Command menu.

Note that the S Pen is sold separately for the Galaxy S23 Ultra, and it needs to be a specific model, called the S Pen Pro, to work with the device's camera.

How to reset the S Pen

To reset the S Pen on a Galaxy S23 Ultra, you can follow these steps:

1. Hold the S Pen button down for about 10 seconds until the S Pen status light blinks twice.

2. Release the button and wait for a few seconds until the light turns off.

3. The S Pen will now be reset, and you can reconnect it to your phone by bringing it close to the device and pressing the button on the pen.

Note that resetting the S Pen will delete all the customized settings and preferences you have set for the pen. If you want to preserve those settings, you can try disconnecting and reconnecting the pen, or clearing the cache and data for the S Pen app in the phone settings.

Changing the color of the S Pen ink

You can change the color of the S Pen ink on a Galaxy S23 Ultra by following these steps:

1. Remove the S Pen from the device and hover the pen over the screen.

2. Tap the button on the S Pen to launch the Air Command menu.

3. Select the **"Pen" tool** from the Air Command menu.

4. At the bottom of the screen, you will see a row of color options. Tap on the color you want to use.

5. Start writing or drawing with the S Pen, and it will use the selected color.

If you want to customize the available colors or create your own, you can do so by opening the **"Settings" app** on your phone, scrolling down to **"S Pen,"** and selecting **"Pen color."** From here, you can add, delete, or rearrange the colors and even create your own custom color by selecting **"Custom color."**

Access S-Pen settings

To access the S Pen settings on a Galaxy S23 Ultra, you can follow these steps:

1. Remove the S Pen from the device and hover the pen over the screen.

2. Tap the button on the S Pen to launch the **Air Command menu**.

3. Tap the settings icon (gear icon) in the lower-right corner of the Air Command menu.

4. This will open the S Pen settings, where you can customize various options such as Air Actions, Pen actions, Pen orientation, Screen off memo, and more.

Alternatively, you can access the S Pen settings by going to the phone's settings app, scrolling down to **"Advanced features,"** and selecting **"S Pen."** From here, you can adjust the S Pen's settings and preferences, including pen sensitivity, sound and vibration, and more.

CHAPTER SEVEN

About Bixby

Bixby is a digital assistant developed by Samsung Electronics for their Android-based smartphones and other devices. The Samsung Galaxy S23 Ultra comes pre-installed with Bixby.

Bixby's primary purpose is to help users execute various tasks on their devices by using either voice commands or touch inputs. It also has the ability to offer personalized suggestions based on a user's preferences and usage habits. Activating Bixby can be done by pressing the dedicated button on the Galaxy S23 Ultra or by simply saying **"Hi, Bixby"** when the device is unlocked.

Aside from basic voice commands like setting alarms, sending messages, and making calls, Bixby also features a function called Bixby Vision. This feature utilizes the device's camera to identify objects and supply information about them, such as recognizing landmarks, translating text, and even facilitating online shopping.

Bixby is a powerful assistant that can assist users in making the most out of their Galaxy S23 Ultra devices. It provides helpful and customized assistance for a variety of tasks.

About Bixby Vision

Bixby Vision is a feature found on Samsung Galaxy S23 Ultra devices that utilizes the device's camera to identify and provide information about objects in real-time. It is an advanced visual assistant that can identify objects, provide translations, and facilitate online shopping.

One of the most notable features of Bixby Vision is its ability to recognize landmarks and provide information about them in real-time. This can be useful for travelers who want to learn more about the places they are visiting. Bixby Vision can also recognize text and translate it into different languages, making it easier for users to communicate when traveling abroad.

Bixby Vision also has a shopping feature that allows users to search for products online using the camera. By pointing the camera at a product, Bixby Vision can search for similar products online, providing users with information about pricing, availability, and reviews.

In addition to these features, Bixby Vision can also recognize wine labels and provide information about the wine, scan QR codes to quickly access information, and identify food items to provide nutritional information.

Overall, Bixby Vision is a powerful feature that enhances the user experience on Samsung Galaxy S23 Ultra devices. It provides users with real-time information about their surroundings, making it easier to identify objects, communicate, and shop.

How to set up Bixby

To set up Bixby on your Galaxy S23 Ultra, follow these steps:

1. Press and hold the Bixby button on the left side of your device or swipe right from the home screen to access Bixby.

2. If this is your first-time using Bixby, you will be prompted to sign in to your Samsung account or create a new one.

3. After signing in or creating an account, you will be prompted to choose your preferred language and agree to the terms and conditions.

4. Next, you will be prompted to enable Bixby Voice. Follow the on-screen instructions to train Bixby to recognize your voice.

5. You can now customize Bixby by selecting your preferred Bixby Home layout, and then adding or removing cards to your liking.

6. You can also customize Bixby by going to the Bixby settings, where you can adjust settings such as wake-up sensitivity and Bixby Vision preferences.

Once you have set up Bixby, you can use it to access a variety of features on your Galaxy S23 Ultra, such as making calls, sending messages, setting reminders, and more. Simply say **"Hi Bixby"** to wake it up and start issuing commands.

How to use Bixby

Bixby on the Galaxy S23 Ultra can be used in various ways, here are some examples:

1. **Voice Commands:** You can use voice commands to perform various tasks, such as calling someone, sending a message, setting

a reminder, playing music, or launching an app. Simply say **"Hi Bixby"** to wake it up, and then issue your command.

2. **Bixby Home:** Bixby Home is a personalized dashboard that displays relevant information based on your preferences and usage history. Swipe right on the home screen to access Bixby Home, where you can see your upcoming events, weather forecast, news, and more.

3. **Bixby Vision:** Bixby Vision uses your device's camera to identify objects, text, and locations. You can use Bixby Vision to translate text, scan QR codes, identify products, and search for images.

4. **Quick Commands:** Quick Commands allow you to create custom voice commands for specific tasks or combinations of tasks. For example, you can create a Quick Command

to send a message to a specific contact with a specific message.

5. **Bixby Routines**: Bixby Routines are a set of automated actions that can be triggered by specific events or situations. For example, you can set up a Bixby Routine to turn on your Wi-Fi when you arrive home, or to turn on your Do Not Disturb mode when you're in a meeting.

To use Bixby, ensure that the Bixby service is enabled in your settings. You can access Bixby settings by opening the Bixby app or by swiping right on the home screen and tapping the settings icon in the top right corner. From there, you can customize Bixby to your liking and access its various features.

How to activate Bixby Vision

Bixby Vision is a feature on the Galaxy S23 Ultra that allows you to use the camera to identify objects, text, and locations, and access various functions such as translation, shopping, and search. To activate Bixby Vision on your Galaxy S23 Ultra, follow these steps:

1. Open the Camera app on your Galaxy S23 Ultra.

2. Swipe left on the camera screen to access Bixby Vision.

3. If this is your first-time using Bixby Vision, you will be prompted to agree to the terms and conditions.

4. Point the camera at an object or text that you want to identify.

5. Bixby Vision will automatically recognize the object or text and display relevant information, such as product details, translation, or search results.

6. You can also use Bixby Vision to scan QR codes, identify landmarks, and search for images.

7. To access more Bixby Vision features, tap the menu icon in the top right corner and select the function you want to use.

Note that Bixby Vision may not work properly in certain lighting or environmental conditions, or if the camera is unable to capture a clear image.

How to use Bixby Vision

Here's how to use Bixby Vision on your Galaxy S23 Ultra:

1. Open the Camera app on your Galaxy S23 Ultra.

2. Swipe left on the camera screen to access Bixby Vision.

3. Point the camera at an object, text, or location that you want to identify.

4. Bixby Vision will automatically recognize the object or text and display relevant information.

5. If Bixby Vision identifies a product, you can tap on the product to see more information, reviews, and price comparisons.

6. If Bixby Vision identifies text, you can tap on the text to translate it, copy it, or search for it.

7. If Bixby Vision identifies a location, you can tap on the location to see more information, such as reviews, directions, and hours of operation.

8. You can also use Bixby Vision to scan QR codes, identify landmarks, and search for images.

9. To access more Bixby Vision features, tap the menu icon in the top right corner and select the function you want to use.

CHAPTER EIGHT

How to use fast-charge and wireless

charging

The Samsung Galaxy S23 Ultra supports both fast charging and wireless charging. Here's how to use each feature:

Fast charging:

1. Make sure you have a compatible fast charger. The Galaxy S23 Ultra supports up to 25W charging, so you'll want a charger that can deliver at least that much power.

2. Connect the fast charger to the phone using a USB-C cable.

3. Your phone should begin charging quickly. You'll see a message on the lock screen indicating that fast charging is enabled.

Wireless charging:

1. Make sure you have a compatible wireless charging pad. The Galaxy S23 Ultra supports both Qi and PMA wireless charging standards.

2. Place the phone on the charging pad, making sure it's centered on the pad.

3. Your phone should begin charging wirelessly. You'll see a message on the lock screen indicating that wireless charging is enabled.

Note that fast charging and wireless charging can't be used simultaneously. If you're using a wireless charger, your phone will charge at the normal wireless charging rate, which is slower than fast charging.

How to use wireless power-sharing

Samsung Galaxy S23 Ultra also supports wireless power-sharing, which allows you to use your phone's battery to charge other devices wirelessly. Here's how to use this feature:

1. Swipe down from the top of the screen to open the notification panel.

2. Tap on the **"Wireless PowerShare" icon**. *(NB: This will open the Wireless PowerShare settings).*

3. Place the device you want to charge face down on a flat surface.

4. Place the back of your Galaxy S23 Ultra on the center of the other device's back. Make sure the two devices are in contact with each other.

5. You should see a message on your phone indicating that power-sharing is enabled. Your phone's battery will begin to charge the other device.

Note that the other device must support wireless charging in order for this feature to work. Also, keep in mind that using wireless power-sharing will drain your phone's battery faster than normal, so it's best to use it sparingly or when you have access to a power source to recharge your phone afterwards.

How to change the Screen Timeout

The screen timeout setting on the Samsung Galaxy S23 Ultra determines how long the screen will remain on before it automatically turns off to save battery life.

Here's how to change the screen timeout:

1. Open the **Settings app** on your phone.

2. Scroll down and tap on **"Display"**.

3. Tap on **"Screen timeout"**.

4. Choose the desired time interval for the screen timeout. *(NB: The options range from 15 seconds to 10 minutes).*

5. Once you've selected the desired screen timeout duration, tap on the back button to save the changes.

Note: Your Galaxy S23 Ultra will now automatically turn off the screen after the selected amount of time has elapsed.

CHAPTER NINE

Voicemail

Voicemail on the Samsung Galaxy S23 Ultra allows you to receive and listen to voice messages left by callers when you are unable to answer the phone. Here's how to set up and use voicemail:

Setting up voicemail:

1. Open the Phone app on your phone.

2. Tap on the three dots in the top-right corner of the screen and select **"Settings".**

3. Scroll down and tap on **"Voicemail".**

4. Tap on **"Set up"** to begin setting up voicemail.

5. Follow the prompts to create a voicemail greeting and set up a PIN. You'll need the PIN to access your voicemail messages.

Using voicemail:

1. When you miss a call, you should receive a notification that you have a new voicemail message. You can also check your voicemail by dialing **"1"** on the Phone app and then following the prompts to enter your PIN.

2. Listen to the voicemail message. You can choose to save, delete, or reply to the message.

3. When you're finished listening to the message, you can hang up the call or choose to listen to more messages.

Note that some carriers may have different voicemail setup procedures, so if the above steps don't work for you, you may need to contact your carrier for assistance.

Navigating through the device using gestures

The Samsung Galaxy S23 Ultra includes a variety of gesture-based navigation options that can help you quickly and easily navigate through the device. Here are some of the most common gestures:

1. **Home screen:** To go to the Home screen, swipe up from the bottom of the screen.

2. **Recent apps:** To see your recent apps, swipe up from the bottom of the screen and hold your finger in the middle of the screen for a moment.

3. **Back button:** To go back to the previous screen, swipe in from the left or right edge of the screen.

4. **Split screen**: To use two apps at the same time, swipe up from the bottom of the screen to see your recent apps, then swipe left or

right on the app you want to use in split screen.

5. **One-handed mode:** To make the screen smaller and easier to reach with one hand, swipe down from the bottom of the screen with your thumb.

6. **Notification panel:** To see your notifications and quick settings, swipe down from the top of the screen.

7. **Quick settings:** To access your quick settings directly from the Home screen, swipe down from the top of the screen with two fingers.

Note that some of these gestures may need to be enabled in the Settings app. To customize your gesture settings, go to **Settings > Display > Navigation bar and gesture**.

Making use of the Navigation bar

The Navigation bar on the Samsung Galaxy S23 Ultra is located at the bottom of the screen and includes several buttons that allow you to navigate through the device. Here are some of the most common ways to use the Navigation bar:

1. **Home button:** This button takes you to the Home screen from anywhere in the device. To use it, simply tap the circle-shaped button in the middle of the Navigation bar.

2. **Back button:** This button allows you to go back to the previous screen or exit an app. To use it, simply tap the left-facing arrow button on the Navigation bar.

3. **Recent apps button:** This button shows you a list of your recently used apps. To use it, simply tap the square-shaped button on the right side of the Navigation bar.

4. **Navigation bar customization:** You can customize the buttons on the Navigation bar to add or remove buttons and change their order. To do this, go to **Settings > Display > Navigation bar and gesture**, and then tap on "Button layout" or "Button order".

5. **Navigation gestures:** If you prefer to use gestures instead of the Navigation bar, you can enable Navigation gestures in the same Settings menu. This will allow you to swipe up from the bottom of the screen to go Home, swipe up and hold to see recent apps, and swipe in from the left or right edge of the screen to go back.

Note that the Navigation bar can be hidden while using some apps or in full-screen mode. To access it again, simply swipe up from the bottom of the screen.

How to change the Navigation bar through Settings

To change the Navigation bar on your Galaxy S23 Ultra, you can follow these steps:

1. Go to the **"Settings" app** on your phone.

2. Tap on **"Display."**

3. Scroll down and tap on **"Navigation Bar."**

4. Here you can customize your Navigation bar by selecting the type of navigation bar you want, changing its color, and adjusting its sensitivity.

5. To change the type of navigation bar, tap on **"Button layout"** and select your desired option.

6. To change the color of the navigation bar, tap on **"Background color"** and select the color you want.

7. To adjust the sensitivity of the navigation bar, tap on **"Touch and hold delay"** and adjust the slider.

Once you have made the desired changes, exit the settings app, and your Navigation bar should reflect the changes you made.

CHAPTER TEN

Camera

The Camera app on the Galaxy S23 Ultra is a powerful and feature-rich application that allows you to take stunning photos and videos. Here are some key features of the Camera app on the Galaxy S23 Ultra:

1. **Pro mode:** The Camera app on the Galaxy S23 Ultra also includes a Pro mode that allows you to manually adjust the camera settings like ISO, shutter speed, and white balance. This gives you greater control over your photos and can help you capture stunning shots in different lighting conditions.

2. **8K video recording:** The Galaxy S23 Ultra also supports 8K video recording, which allows you

to capture high-resolution videos with amazing detail.

3. **Night mode:** The Camera app on the Galaxy S23 Ultra also includes a Night mode, which uses advanced algorithms to capture clear and bright photos in low-light conditions.

4. **Single Take:** The Single Take feature allows you to capture multiple photos and videos with just one click. The Camera app will automatically capture a variety of shots, including photos, videos, and even boomerang-style animations.

Overall, the Camera app on the Galaxy S23 Ultra is a powerful and versatile application that allows you to capture stunning photos and videos with ease.

How to view and edit photos

To view and edit photos on your Samsung Galaxy S23 Ultra, follow these steps:

1. Open the Gallery app on your phone. This app should come pre-installed on your device.

2. Browse through your photos to find the one you want to view or edit.

3. To view a photo, simply tap on it. You can then swipe left or right to view other photos in the same album.

4. To edit a photo, tap on the photo you want to edit and then tap on the Edit button at the bottom of the screen.

5. You can now make various adjustments to the photo, such as cropping, adjusting the brightness and contrast, adding filters, and more. Once you have made your changes, tap on Save to save your edited photo.

6. If you want to revert your changes and restore the original photo, tap on Revert.

7. You can also share your photos directly from the Gallery app by tapping on the Share button at the bottom of the screen. From here, you can select the method you want to use to share your photo, such as via email, social media, or messaging apps.

With these simple steps, you can view and edit your photos on your Samsung Galaxy S23 Ultra with ease.

How to play and edit videos

To play videos on your Samsung Galaxy S23 Ultra, follow these steps:

1. Open the Gallery app on your device.

2. Tap on the video you want to play.

3. Tap on the **Play icon** to start playing the video.

To edit videos on your Samsung Galaxy S23 Ultra, follow these steps:

1. Open the Gallery app on your device.

2. Tap on the video you want to edit.

3. Tap on the **Edit icon** (it looks like a pencil).

4. You can now edit the video using the available tools, such as trimming, adding filters, and adjusting the speed.

5. Once you have finished editing the video, tap on the Save or Save as button to save your changes.

Note: If you want more advanced video editing features, you can download a third-party video editing app from the Google Play Store.

How to share videos and photos

To share videos and photos from your Samsung Galaxy S23 Ultra, you can follow these steps:

1. Open the Gallery app on your Samsung Galaxy S23 Ultra.

2. Select the video or photo you want to share.

3. Tap the share icon, which looks like a curved arrow pointing to the right.

4. Choose the app or method you want to use to share the video or photo. Some common options include:

- **Messaging**: Send the video or photo in a text message to someone.

- **Email:** Send the video or photo as an email attachment.

- **Bluetooth:** Share the video or photo directly with another Bluetooth-enabled device.

- **Social media:** Post the video or photo to a social media app like Facebook or Instagram.

- **Nearby Share:** Use Google's Nearby Share feature to share the video or photo with another nearby Android device.

- **Samsung Quick Share:** Use Samsung's Quick Share feature to share the video or photo with another nearby Samsung device.

5. Follow the prompts to complete the sharing process. Depending on the app or method you choose, you may need to select a recipient or destination, add a message or caption, and adjust other settings.

Once you've completed these steps, your video or photo will be shared with the recipient or destination you selected.

How to delete videos and photos

To delete videos and photos on your Galaxy S23 Ultra, follow these steps:

1. Open the Gallery app on your Galaxy S23 Ultra.

2. Select the photo or video you want to delete.

3. Tap the trash can icon located at the bottom of the screen.

4. Confirm that you want to delete the photo or video by tapping **"Delete."**

Alternatively, you can select multiple photos or videos to delete at once by following these steps:

1. Open the Gallery app on your Galaxy S23 Ultra.

2. Tap and hold the first photo or video you want to delete.

3. Tap on the other photos or videos you want to delete.

4. Tap the trash can icon located at the bottom of the screen.

5. Confirm that you want to delete the selected photos or videos by tapping **"Delete."**

Note that once you delete a photo or video, it cannot be recovered unless you have a backup of the file.

How to record a Slo-mo video

To record a slow-motion video on your Samsung Galaxy S23 Ultra, follow these steps:

1. Open the Camera app on your Samsung Galaxy S23 Ultra.

2. Swipe left on the camera modes to select **"Slow motion".**

3. Tap the record button to start recording your video.

4. You can adjust the speed of the slow-motion effect by tapping the speed icon on the left side of the screen.

5. Tap the stop button to end the recording.

6. The slow-motion video will be saved to your phone's gallery.

Note: The slow-motion feature on the Samsung Galaxy S23 Ultra supports up to 960 frames per second, which can capture very slow-motion footage.

Making use of the Live Focus feature

The Live Focus feature on the Samsung Galaxy S23 Ultra allows you to take photos with a blurred background, which can make the subject stand out and look more professional. Here's how to use the Live Focus feature:

1. Open the **Camera app** on your Samsung Galaxy S23 Ultra.

2. Swipe left on the camera modes to select **"Live Focus".**

3. Aim your camera at the subject you want to photograph.

4. The camera will automatically detect the subject and blur the background.

5. Tap the shutter button to take the photo.

6. You can adjust the amount of blur using the slider at the bottom of the screen, or choose different blur styles using the icons above the slider.

7. Once you're happy with the photo, tap the **save button** to save it to your phone's gallery.

Note: Live Focus works best when there is a clear distinction between the subject and the background, so it may not work well in all lighting conditions or with all subjects.

How to use night mode

The night mode feature on the Samsung Galaxy S23 Ultra helps you capture better photos in low-light conditions. Here's how to use it:

1. Open the Camera app on your Samsung Galaxy S23 Ultra.

2. Swipe left on the camera modes to select **"Night mode"**.

3. Aim your camera at the subject you want to photograph.

4. Hold your phone steady for a few seconds to allow the camera to capture multiple frames and combine them into one brighter and clearer photo.

5. Once the photo is captured, you can adjust the brightness and other settings using the editing tools at the bottom of the screen.

6. Tap the save button to save the photo to your phone's gallery.

Note: Night mode works best when there is very little light, so it may not work well in well-lit environments. Also, using night mode may take longer to capture the photo, so it's important to hold your phone steady until the process is complete.

How to use the Zoom feature

The Samsung Galaxy S23 Ultra has a powerful zoom feature that allows you to zoom in on distant subjects without losing image quality. Here's how to use it:

1. Open the **Camera app** on your Samsung Galaxy S21 Ultra.

2. Swipe up or down on the screen to zoom in or out.

3. Alternatively, you can use the pinch-to-zoom gesture to zoom in or out.

4. You can also use the zoom slider at the bottom of the screen to adjust the level of zoom.

5. If you want to switch to the ultra-wide lens, tap the ultra-wide icon on the left side of the screen.

6. To switch back to the main lens, tap the 1x icon on the screen.

Note: The zoom feature on the Samsung Galaxy S23 Ultra has both optical and digital zoom. Optical zoom provides better image quality and clarity compared to digital zoom, which can reduce image quality. It's recommended to use optical zoom whenever possible.

CHAPTER ELEVEN

How to use AR Doodle

AR Doodle is a fun feature that lets you draw in 3D space using the camera on your Galaxy S23 Ultra.

Here's how to use it:

1. Open the camera app on your Galaxy S23 Ultra.

2. Swipe left on the camera modes until you see **"AR Doodle."**

3. Tap **"AR Doodle"** to enter the mode.

4. Once in AR Doodle mode, you'll see a blank canvas in front of you. You can start drawing by tapping the pen icon at the bottom of the screen.

5. Choose a color and brush size, and then draw in 3D space. Your doodle will stay in place even if you move the camera around.

6. You can also use the eraser tool to remove parts of your doodle.

7. If you want to add a new doodle, tap the plus sign icon to create a new canvas.

8. When you're finished, you can take a photo or record a video of your AR Doodle by tapping the camera or video icon.

AR Doodle is a fun way to add some creativity to your photos and videos. Give it a try and see what kind of doodles you can come up with.

How to use PENUP

PENUP is an app for Galaxy S23 Ultra that allows you to draw and share your artwork with other PENUP users.

Here's how to use it:

1. Open the PENUP app on your Galaxy S23 Ultra.

2. If it's your first time using PENUP, you'll need to create an account. You can sign up with your Samsung account or create a new one.

3. Once you're logged in, you can start drawing. You can choose from a variety of drawing tools, including pencils, markers, brushes, and more. You can also select different colors and adjust the size and opacity of your tool.

4. If you're not sure what to draw, you can browse through the community feed to see what other PENUP users have created. You can also join challenges and contests to show off your skills.

5. When you're finished with your drawing, you can share it with the PENUP community by tapping the **"Upload" button**. You can add a

title, description, and tags to help other users find your artwork.

6. You can also save your drawing to your device or share it on social media.

PENUP is a great way to explore your creativity and connect with other artists. Give it a try and see what kind of artwork you can create

How to adjust keyboard settings

You can adjust the keyboard settings on your Galaxy S23 Ultra to customize the keyboard to your preferences. Here's how to do it:

1. Open the Settings app on your Galaxy S23 Ultra.

2. Tap **"General management"** and then **"Language and input."**

3. Tap **"On-screen keyboard"** and then select **"Samsung Keyboard."**

4. In the Samsung Keyboard settings, you can adjust a variety of settings, including:

- **Keyboard layout:** Choose between standard, floating, or split keyboard layouts.

- **Keyboard size and transparency:** Adjust the size of the keyboard and the transparency level.

- **Key-tap feedback**: Turn on or off sound and vibration feedback when you type.

- **Auto-capitalization and spacing:** Enable or disable automatic capitalization and spacing between words.

- **Language and input:** Add or remove languages and adjust the input methods for each language.

- **Text shortcuts:** Create and manage text shortcuts for frequently used phrases.

- **Swipe typing:** Enable or disable swipe typing, and adjust the swipe trail color and thickness.

- **Predictive text:** Adjust the predictive text settings, including word suggestions and auto-correction.

5. Once you've made your desired adjustments, you can exit the Samsung Keyboard settings.

By adjusting the keyboard settings on your Galaxy S23 Ultra, you can create a typing experience that works best for you.

How to use keyboard

The keyboard on your Galaxy S23 Ultra is a standard QWERTY keyboard that you can use to type messages, emails, and other text. Here's how to use it:

1. Open an app where you can type, such as Messages or Email.

2. Tap the text field to bring up the keyboard.

3. Use your fingers to tap the keys on the keyboard to type your message. The keys are arranged in the standard QWERTY layout, with letters, numbers, and symbols.

4. If you make a mistake while typing, you can use the backspace key to delete the last character you typed.

5. You can also use the shift key to capitalize letters, and the arrow keys to move the cursor to different parts of your text.

6. If you need to enter special characters or symbols, you can access them by tapping the **"123" key**, or by tapping and holding certain keys to bring up alternate characters.

7. You can also use swipe typing by sliding your finger across the keyboard to spell out words, without having to lift your finger from the screen.

8. Once you've finished typing your message, you can tap the send button to send it.

Note: The keyboard on your Galaxy S23 Ultra is easy to use and comes with a variety of settings and features that you can customize to your preferences.

How to copy, paste, and delete text

Copying, pasting, and deleting text is a common task when using a keyboard on your Galaxy S23 Ultra. Here's how to do it:

Copying text:

1. Press and hold the text you want to copy until it's highlighted.

2. Tap **"Copy"** from the menu that appears. The selected text will be copied to your clipboard.

Pasting text:

1. Place your cursor where you want to paste the copied text.

2. Press and hold the text field until the **"Paste" option** appears.

3. Tap **"Paste"** to paste the copied text into the field.

Deleting text:

1. Place your cursor where you want to delete text.

2. Use the backspace key to delete the text to the left of the cursor.

3. Alternatively, you can select the text you want to delete by pressing and holding on it until it's highlighted, and then tapping the **"Delete" button** that appears.

Note: These actions may vary depending on the app you are using. Some apps may have their own unique method for copying, pasting, and deleting text.

CHAPTER TWELVE

How to take screenshots

To take a screenshot on a Samsung Galaxy S23 Ultra, you can use any of the following methods:

Method 1: Using hardware buttons

1. Navigate to the screen you want to capture.

2. Press and hold the **Volume Down button and the Power button** simultaneously for a few seconds.

3. Release both buttons when you see a flash on the screen, or hear a camera shutter sound.

4. The screenshot will be saved to your device's gallery.

Method 2: Using palm swipe gesture

1. Ensure that Palm swipe to capture is enabled. To do this, go to **Settings > Advanced features > Motions and gestures > Palm swipe** to capture, and toggle the switch to enable it.

2. Navigate to the screen you want to capture.

3. Place the side of your hand on the screen and swipe it from left to right or right to left.

4. The screenshot will be saved to your device's gallery.

Method 3: Using Bixby Voice command

1. Ensure that Bixby Voice is enabled. To do this, press and hold the Power button, and then tap the Bixby Voice icon.

2. Navigate to the screen you want to capture.

3. Say **"Hey Bixby, take a screenshot."**

4. The screenshot will be saved to your device's gallery.

You can access your screenshots in the Gallery app, and from there, you can edit and share them as desired.

How to activate screen recording

To activate screen recording on a Samsung Galaxy S23 Ultra, you can use the following steps:

1. Swipe down from the top of the screen to open the Notification panel.

2. Look for the Screen recorder icon and tap it to open the Screen recorder settings. If you don't see the icon, you can add it by tapping the three dots on the top right corner of the screen, selecting **"Button order"**, and then dragging the Screen recorder icon to the Quick settings panel.

3. In the Screen recorder settings, you can customize the video quality, audio settings, and other options. You can also enable or

disable the microphone and the front camera.

4. Once you're ready to start recording, tap the Screen recorder icon in the Quick settings panel.

5. A countdown will begin, and then the recording will start. You can pause and resume the recording as needed by tapping the Screen recorder icon.

6. To stop the recording, swipe down from the top of the screen and tap the Stop icon in the notification panel.

7. The screen recording will be saved to your device's gallery, where you can edit and share it as desired.

Enable One-Handed mode

To enable and use One-Handed mode on a Samsung Galaxy S23 Ultra, you can follow these steps:

1. Open the **Settings app**.

2. Tap on **Advanced features**.

3. Tap on **One-Handed mode**.

4. Toggle on the switch for the feature.

5. Choose the type of gesture you want to use to activate One-Handed mode.

6. Choose the size of the screen you want to use in One-Handed mode. You can choose from three different sizes.

7. Once you have enabled One-Handed mode, you can activate it by performing the gesture you selected in step 5.

8. When activated, the screen will shrink to the size you selected in step 6, making it easier to use with one hand.

9. You can adjust the position of the shrunken screen by swiping up or down on the bar at the bottom of the screen.

10.   To exit One-Handed mode, tap on the black area outside of the shrunken screen.

Note: The steps for enabling and using One-Handed mode may vary slightly depending on the specific version of Android and the Samsung One UI that is installed on your device.

Activate Dark Mode

To activate and use Dark Mode on a Samsung Galaxy S23 Ultra, you can use the following steps:

1. Open the Settings app.

2. Tap on **Display**.

3. Tap on **Dark mode**.

4. Toggle on the switch for Dark mode.

5. You can choose to have Dark mode turn on automatically at sunset and turn off at sunrise by enabling the **"Turn on as scheduled" option**.

6. You can also choose to have specific apps use Dark mode by tapping on **"Dark mode settings for individual apps"**.

7. To use Dark mode, simply navigate to any app or screen, and the background will be black instead of white.

8. To turn off Dark mode, follow the same steps and toggle off the switch for Dark mode.

Note: Some apps may not support Dark mode, so they may still have a white background even if Dark mode is turned on.

CHAPTER THIRTEEN

Phone App

The Phone app on the Galaxy S23 Ultra is a pre-installed application that allows you to make and receive phone calls, send and receive text messages, and manage your contacts. It also includes features such as call waiting, caller ID, and voicemail.

Additionally, the Phone app on the Galaxy S23 Ultra may have other features and settings unique to Samsung devices, such as spam protection and call blocking. You can customize these features and settings to suit your preferences through the app's settings menu.

Overall, the Phone app is an essential tool for communication on the Galaxy S23 Ultra, and it is a reliable and intuitive application that can help you stay connected with friends, family, and colleagues.

Making a phone call

Here's how you can make a phone call on the Galaxy S23 Ultra:

1. **Open the Phone app:** You can find the Phone app on the home screen or in the app drawer. Tap on the Phone icon to open the app.

2. **Dial the number:** Use the keypad to enter the phone number you want to call. If the number is saved in your contacts, you can search for the contact and tap on the name to call them.

3. **Press the Call button:** Once you have entered the phone number or selected a contact, tap on the green Call button to start the call.

Alternatively, you can use voice commands to make a call by saying **"Hey Google" or "Hi Bixby"** followed by the name of the contact or the phone number you want to call.

During the call, you can adjust the volume, mute the call, or use the speakerphone option by tapping on the corresponding icons on the call screen. You can also add another call, merge calls, or put the current call on hold to answer another call by tapping on the corresponding options on the call screen. When the call is over, tap on the **red End Call button** to hang up.

How to receive and decline a call

To receive a call on the Samsung Galaxy S23 Ultra, you can follow these steps:

1. When you receive a call, you will see the caller ID on your phone screen.

2. To answer the call, swipe the green phone icon to the right or press the **green "Answer" button.**

3. Alternatively, you can also answer the call by pressing the volume up button or the power button twice.

To decline a call on the Samsung Galaxy S23 Ultra, you can follow these steps:

1. When you receive a call, you will see the caller ID on your phone screen.

2. To decline the call, swipe the red phone icon to the left or press the **red "Decline" button.**

3. Alternatively, you can also decline the call by pressing the volume down button or the power button once.

How to send Messages

To send a message on a Samsung Galaxy S23 Ultra, follow these steps:

1. Open the **Messaging app** on your Galaxy S23 Ultra.

2. Tap the **compose button** (the pencil icon in the bottom right corner).

3. Select the recipient by typing their name or phone number in the "To" field.

4. Enter your message in the text field at the bottom of the screen.

5. When you're ready to send the message, tap the send button (the arrow icon in the text field).

Alternatively, you can also use voice commands to send messages. To do this, you can say **"Hey Google"** to activate Google Assistant, and then say **"Send a message to [contact name]"** followed by your message. Google Assistant will then confirm the recipient and message before sending it for you.

Note that you will need to have an active cellular connection or Wi-Fi connection to send messages. If you're experiencing issues with sending messages, make sure your phone is connected to a network and that your messaging app settings are configured correctly.

How to delete and pin conversations

To delete a conversation on a Samsung Galaxy S23 Ultra, follow these steps:

1. Open the Messaging app on your Galaxy S23 Ultra.

2. Find the conversation you want to delete.

3. Long-press on the conversation until a menu appears.

4. Tap **"Delete"** or the trash can icon.

5. Confirm that you want to delete the conversation.

To pin a conversation on a Samsung Galaxy S23 Ultra, follow these steps:

1. Open the **Messaging app** on your Galaxy S23 Ultra.

2. Find the conversation you want to pin.

3. Long-press on the conversation until a menu appears.

4. Tap **"Pin conversation"** or the pin icon.

5. The conversation will now appear at the top of your messaging app, marked with a pin icon.

Note that deleting a conversation will permanently remove it from your device, so be sure you want to delete it before doing so. Pinned conversations will remain at the top of your messaging app until you unpin them, even if you receive new messages from other contacts.

How to send SOS messages

To send an SOS message on a Samsung Galaxy S23 Ultra, follow these steps:

1. Open the Settings app on your Galaxy S21 Ultra.

2. Scroll down and tap **"Advanced features."**

3. Tap **"Send SOS messages."**

4. Toggle on **"Send SOS messages."**

5. If desired, you can also toggle on **"Attach pictures"** or **"Attach audio recording"** to include additional information in your SOS message.

6. You can also choose up to four emergency contacts to receive your SOS message. Tap

"Add" next to "Emergency contacts" and select the contact you want to add.

7. Once you have set up your SOS message settings, press the power button three times to send an SOS message.

The SOS message will include your current location, a picture (if you included one), a 5-second audio recording (if you included one), and a message stating that you need help. Your selected emergency contacts will receive the message and your location information so that they can help you.

Note that you must have a cellular or Wi-Fi connection and have location services turned on for the SOS message to work properly.

How to block annoying messages

To block annoying messages on a Samsung Galaxy S23 Ultra, follow these steps:

1. Open the Messaging app on your Galaxy S23 Ultra.

2. Find the conversation from the sender you want to block.

3. Long-press on the conversation until a menu appears.

4. Tap **"Block"** or the **"Block number" option**.

5. Confirm that you want to block the sender.

Alternatively, block a sender from the phone's Settings app. Here's how:

1. Open the Settings app on your Galaxy S23 Ultra.

2. Scroll down and tap **"Apps."**

3. Find and tap on the Messaging app.

4. Tap **"Permissions."**

5. Tap **"SMS" or "MMS"** (depending on the type of message you want to block).

6. Scroll down and tap **"Block messages."**

7. Toggle on **"Block unknown senders"** to block messages from anyone not in your contacts list.

8. Tap **"Block numbers"** to manually enter or select a number from your recent calls or contacts list.

Once you've blocked a sender, their messages will no longer appear in your messaging app. You will not receive notifications from their messages, and they cannot contact you through text messages.

Note that blocking a sender is a good way to stop receiving annoying messages, but it does not prevent them from contacting you through other means, such as phone calls or social media.

CHAPTER FOURTEEN

Basic troubleshooting issues

The Samsung Galaxy S23 Ultra is one of the most advanced smartphones on the market, with cutting-edge features and top-of-the-line performance. However, even the best devices can experience issues from time to time, and the Galaxy S23 Ultra is no exception. Here, we will discuss some of the most common troubleshooting issues that users may encounter with their Galaxy S23 Ultra and how to resolve them.

1. **Battery Drain Issues**: One of the most common issues Galaxy S23 Ultra users face is battery drain. This issue can be frustrating, especially if you rely heavily on your device throughout the day. There are several reasons why your phone may be experiencing battery drain, including background apps, display settings,

and faulty hardware. To troubleshoot this issue, follow these steps:

- Check the battery usage in the settings to see which apps use the most.

- Turn off features like **Always-On Display and adaptive brightness**, which can drain the battery quickly.

- Disable unnecessary background processes by going to **Settings > Device Care > Battery > App power management.**

- Restart your phone, which can help refresh the system and clear out any background processes draining the battery.

- It may be a hardware issue if none of the above steps work. In this case, you may need to replace the battery or have the phone repaired.

2. **Overheating Issues:** Another common issue that Galaxy S23 Ultra users experience is

overheating. This can happen when the device is used for extended periods or with intensive gaming or video streaming applications. Overheating can cause the phone to shut down or damage the internal components. To troubleshoot this issue, follow these steps:

- Remove the phone case and allow the phone to cool down for a few minutes.

- Turn off unused features and applications to reduce the workload on the processor.

- Avoid using the phone in direct sunlight or hot environments.

- Restart your phone, which can help to refresh the system and clear out any background processes that may be causing the overheating.

- If the problem persists, there may be a hardware issue. In this case, you may need to have the phone repaired.

3. **Slow Performance:** If your Galaxy S23 Ultra is running slowly or freezing up, it may be due to several factors, including a lack of storage space, outdated software, or a virus or malware infection. To troubleshoot this issue, follow these steps:

- Clear the cache on your phone by going to **Settings > Apps > Clear cache**.

- Uninstall any unnecessary applications that may be taking up storage space.

- Ensure your phone's software is up-to-date by going to **Settings > Software update > Download and install.**

- Run a virus scan using a reputable antivirus application.

- Restart your phone, which can help refresh the system and clear out any background processes causing the slow performance.

4. **Connectivity Issues:** Connectivity issues are another common problem that Galaxy S23 Ultra users may encounter. This can include problems with Wi-Fi, Bluetooth, and cellular data. To troubleshoot these issues, follow these steps:

- For Wi-Fi issues, ensure your phone is within the network range and the correct password has been entered. You can also try restarting your phone or resetting the network settings by going to **Settings > General management > Reset > Reset network settings.**

- For Bluetooth issues, ensure the device you are trying to connect to is within range and that Bluetooth is turned on. You can also try restarting your phone or resetting the Bluetooth settings by going to **Settings > Connections > Bluetooth > Advanced > Reset.**

- Make sure your phone is in an area with good network coverage and that cellular data is turned on for cellular data issues.

How to update your software

To update the software on your Galaxy S23 Ultra, follow these steps:

1. Go to the **"Settings" app** on your phone.

2. Scroll down and select **"Software update."**

3. Click on **"Download and install"** to check for any available updates.

4. If an update is available, click **"Download and install"** again to start the update process.

5. Wait for the download to complete, then click **"Install now"** to install the update.

6. Your phone will restart automatically after the update is installed.

Note: It's recommended to have your phone charged above 50% or plugged into a power source during the update process. Also, it's best to have a stable internet connection to ensure a smooth download and installation process.

How to reset the network

To reset the network settings on your Galaxy S23 Ultra, follow these steps:

1. Go to the **"Settings" app** on your phone.

2. Scroll down and select **"General management"**.

3. Click on **"Reset"** at the bottom of the page.

4. Select **"Reset network settings"** from the options.

5. Click on **"Reset settings"** to confirm.

6. Enter your phone's security PIN, password, or pattern if prompted.

7. Click on **"Reset" again** to confirm.

8. Wait for the reset process to complete, and then restart your phone.

After the restart, your network settings will be restored to their default settings. After the reset, you will need to reconnect to your Wi-Fi networks, Bluetooth devices, and mobile networks.

How to reset factory data

To reset the Galaxy S23 Ultra to its factory data, please follow these steps:

1. Open the **"Settings" app** on your device.

2. Scroll down and tap on **"General management."**

3. Tap on **"Reset"** near the bottom of the page.

4. Select **"Factory data reset."**

5. Scroll down and tap on **"Reset."**

6. If prompted, enter your password or PIN.

7. Tap on **"Delete all"** to confirm the reset.

Note that this will erase all data on your phone, including apps, contacts, and media, so back up anything important before proceeding. Once the reset is complete, you must go through the initial setup process again to set up your device.

Tips for using Samsung Galaxy S23 Ultra

The Galaxy S23 Ultra is a high-end smartphone offering various features and functions. Here are some tips and tricks to help you get the most out of your device.

1. **Customize your home screen:** The Galaxy S23 Ultra allows you to customize your home screen with various widgets, app icons, and wallpapers. To access the customization options, press and hold the home screen and select **"Home screen settings."** You can add or

remove app icons, change the wallpaper, and add widgets from here.

2. **Use Samsung DeX:** Samsung DeX is a feature allows you to connect your Galaxy S23 Ultra to a monitor, keyboard, and mouse, effectively turning it into a desktop computer. To use Samsung DeX, connect your phone to a monitor using a USB-C to HDMI adapter, and then connect a keyboard and mouse to your phone via Bluetooth. You can then use your phone as a touchpad and start using your phone as a desktop computer.

3. **Use the camera's pro mode:** The Galaxy S23 Ultra's camera comes with a pro mode that allows you to manually adjust the camera settings to get the perfect shot. To access the pro mode, open the camera app, swipe to the left to access the camera modes, and select **"Pro."** From here, you can adjust settings such as ISO, shutter speed, and white balance to get the perfect shot.

4. **Use the Edge panels:** The Galaxy S23 Ultra comes with Edge panels that allow you to quickly access your favorite apps, contacts, and tools. To access the Edge panels, swipe in from the right side of the screen. You can customize the Edge panels by going to **"Settings" > "Display" > "Edge panels."**

5. **Use the One-handed mode:** If you find it difficult to use your Galaxy S23 Ultra with one hand, you can enable the One-handed mode. To enable One-handed mode, go to **"Settings" > "Advanced features" > "One-handed mode."** From here, you can reduce the screen size, shift the keyboard to one side, or enable gesture controls.

6. **Use the Samsung Pay feature**: The Galaxy S23 Ultra comes with Samsung Pay, a mobile payment service that allows you to pay for goods and services using your phone. To use Samsung Pay, simply swipe up from the bottom of the screen and select the card you

want to use. In addition, you can add your credit or debit cards to Samsung Pay by going to **"Settings" > "Biometrics and security" > "Samsung Pay."**

7. **Use the Bixby assistant:** The Galaxy S23 Ultra comes with Bixby, a virtual assistant that can help you perform various tasks, such as setting reminders, sending messages, and making calls. To access Bixby, press and hold the Bixby button on the phone's left side or swipe to the right on the home screen. You can customize Bixby by going to **"Settings" > "Advanced features" > "Bixby Routines."**

8. **Use the Secure Folder feature:** The Galaxy S23 Ultra has the Secure Folder feature, allowing you to keep your sensitive files and apps secure. To access Secure Folder, go to **"Settings" > "Biometrics and security" > "Secure Folder."** From here, you can add files, apps, and contacts to Secure Folder and set up a lock method.

9. **Use the Always-on display feature:** The Galaxy S23 Ultra has an Always-on display feature that lets you see the time, date, and notifications without unlocking your phone. To customize the Always-on display, go to **"Settings" > "Lock screen" > "Always On Display."** You can choose the clock style, display mode, and schedule from here.

10. **Add Smart Widgets**

One of the impressive features of the Galaxy S23 Ultra is the inclusion of Smart Widgets on the Home Screen. With this feature, you can gather all your favorite apps in a single space on your device.

- Add Smart Widgets
- Hold an empty area on the Home Screen and click on the Widgets toggle that shows up.
- Click on **Smart Widgets** and then select any one of the options displayed.

Using Samsung Health

Here are the steps you can follow to use Samsung Health on a Galaxy S23 Ultra:

1. Launch the Samsung Health app on your Galaxy S23 Ultra. You can find the app in the app drawer or home screen.

2. You'll be asked to sign in or create a Samsung account when you first launch the app. If you don't have a Samsung account, you can create one by following the on-screen instructions.

3. Once you've signed in, you'll be taken to the Samsung Health home screen. You can access various app features from here, such as the step tracker, workout tracker, and sleep tracker.

4. To use a specific feature, simply tap on it. For example, if you want to track your steps, tap

on the **"Step tracker" icon**. If you want to track your workouts, tap the **"Workout tracker" icon.**

5. Once you've started tracking your activity, you can view your progress and statistics by going back to the Samsung Health home screen and tapping the relevant section.

6. You can also customize the app by going to the settings menu. You can change your goals, adjust notifications, and manage your connected devices here.

Overall, Samsung Health is a comprehensive health and fitness app that can help you track your activity, monitor your progress, and achieve your fitness goals. Following the steps outlined above, you can use Samsung Health on your Galaxy S23 Ultra and take advantage of all its features.

CONCLUSION

In comparison to its highly regarded predecessor, the Galaxy S23 Ultra features several significant upgrades, the most notable of which are a chip that is more powerful and efficient, an improved camera system, increased storage space that is both faster and more accessible, faster RAM, and protection provided by Gorilla Glass Victus 2.

Don't forget that the device still comes with an integrated S Pen, that the Samsung Knox security system safeguards it, and that it provides four years of major OS upgrades and five years of security updates.

When everything is said and done, the Galaxy S23 Ultra is an example of Samsung taking a step in the right way. It is not a revolutionary change, but it does improve in all the main aspects. It has an excellent new processor (that eventually comes to all customers), greater audio quality, twice the storage, an improved design, and a more powerful camera. These are the kinds of items that everyone will value.

Even though they are far less significant, the remainder of the small adjustments are also excellent additions: The enhancements in video stabilization are once again excellent, but they will not affect the game's dynamic. 8K footage is still not something that many people would use.

ABOUT THE AUTHOR

Ernest Woodruff is an American-born tech expert and has bagged a series of praises and acknowledgements for his selfless service to the technology world. His determination and drive for a better tech world has led to his tech writings and blogs. His commitment is also being applauded in the books he has written so far. His notable achievements have been acknowledged by other top technological experts in other countries. With the technological world gradually improving and advancing by the day, the American-born tech expert is sure to leave more legacies for the living and the unborn ones.

Made in United States
Troutdale, OR
12/03/2023

15269677R00108